ARTS AND CRAFTS
MEDIA IDEAS
FOR THE
ELEMENTARY
TEACHER

ARTS AND CRAFTS
MEDIA IDEAS
FOR THE
ELEMENTARY
TEACHER

Ireene Robbins

Parker Publishing Company, Inc.
West Nyack, New York

Library of Congress Cataloging in Publication Data

Robbins, Ireene.
   Arts and crafts media ideas for the elementary
teacher.

   1. Art—Study and teaching (Elementary)
I. Title.
N350.R54   372.5'044   73-8803
ISBN 0-13-047050-3

DEDICATED TO JULIA WEBER GORDON

MY TEACHER AND MENTOR

A Word from the Author

One of the major concerns of a classroom teacher should be to provide the class with a comprehensive program in art. The program should be a sequence of learning experiences that are scheduled and planned; for using a familiar medium in a new and different way will add further interest to the art lesson. However, the main thrust should center on motivation of a subjective nature. Clever techniques should be used to supplement stimulation in any given art lesson. The learning of techniques is essential at any age, nevertheless; and the knowledge of them should act as an aid to further creative productivity.

Chances are, when you were in elementary school art was taught in drawing and painting lessons that duplicated realism. You may say, "I have never been prepared to teach art, and I have little or no help." If this be the case, let us consider logical assistance for you, the classroom teacher. First, the teacher does not have to be an artist in order to lead, motivate and stimulate children when doing an art activity. The role of the teacher is to act as a guide and to offer encouragement when needed during the lesson.

This guide lists innumerable ideas that will help the teacher satisfy the need for variations in the art program within the limits of time and material at her disposal. It was designed as a working tool for the teacher. Many basic media are described in detail and realistic projects are suggested for easy use. The book is structured to familiarize the unfamiliar through various techniques and art media. It suggests ways to implement materials in easily defined practices.

Crayon, dyes, ink, graphics, paint, pencil, paper, pastels, plastic foam, string, textiles and wire are explored fully with tested lessons to make each experience a happy one. There are enough creative lessons listed in the guide to stimulate the teacher's and students' inventiveness for many profitable hours; however, they are not planned to dominate the art program, rather to supplement it.

7

For a number of years, I was involved in Teacher Training Art Workshops. The classroom teachers would request over and over that we offer them ideas and help in using various media — ideas that could be used in the classroom by the classroom teacher, and ideas that included materials and media that were available. Ideas and media techniques are offered here in simple, understandable language. Teachers can set into motion an interesting and exciting sequential program without feeling uncertain and frustrated in their attempts to teach an art lesson effectively.

Creating art is part of the normal development of boys and girls. They love to create and should be encouraged and guided by the teacher through all types of art experiences and opportunities. Every teacher has the opportunity to help the child develop his innate talent so that he may grow up to be a creative, sensitive person who will respond to his fellow man and his environment with aesthetic appreciation. This is an exciting challenge to both the teacher and the child, and both can gain from the spontaneity of ideas that creative art engenders.

Suggestions of an unfamiliar nature can be found throughout this book pertaining to all phases of art endeavor, materials and tools. Along with these ideas there are special sections on How to Use This Book, Hints, Suggestions and Recipes, and many illustrations relating to the various media ideas discussed. Also, there is a Glossary at the end of the book to aid the reader in understanding some of the art terminology used, and the terms that are defined in the Glossary are highlighted in *italics* in the text for easy reference.

This book does not promise to make the reader an art specialist. However, it does suggest that you attempt some of its lessons and tear down the old image that art is meant for a privileged, "talented" few. With this in mind, begin to explore the various media and ideas of the art world with your students. You will find that they will lead to many creative and wonderful classroom experiences.

Ireene Robbins

How to Use This Book

The author has attempted to touch on most of the art media, old and new, that is used in the classroom today. There are innumerable ideas listed in the text, and they are all planned to make every art lesson a creative adventure.

Because the book offers such a wide variety of suggestions, the reader may find it difficult to make a decision regarding the type of medium in which to begin. Listed below are a number of possibilities that will aid the reader in planning a successful and gratifying art experience. Art work is fun to do, and all the hazards that one fears can be remedied through practice. Always do a sample of the particular lesson that is being planned beforehand.

- Before starting a project, peruse the book thoroughly and choose a medium that you find particularly stimulating.
- Then decide upon a particular project in that area and read the material-requirement list thoroughly.
- Gather together all the supplies required for the project.
- Now find a good working area with ample space, and prepare the area for the working procedure.
- Newspaper is an excellent cover for the work area: It is easily acquired and can be disposed of quickly and efficiently when the work is concluded. It also offers an area on which to experiment with the medium before using it on the prepared working surface.
- Place the supplies in an easily accessible area of the room so they can be manipulated with little effort, and so the work plan will run smoothly.
- Before beginning the project, reread the directions so the plan of operation is clear in the reader's mind. (If possible, have the book open to the page of directions being used, and place the book close by so that it can be referred to when necessary.)

• If you feel better protected with a smock, wear one. An old shirt minus sleeves makes an excellent cover-all for young and old.
• Now proceed with the lesson. Work with confidence. Art work is not to be feared.

One last bit of advice: It is imperative that the teacher or group leader do a preliminary test run of the project that is being planned for future use. This assures success because possible problems can be anticipated before they occur during the plan of operation.

Many other suggestions might be made concerning the various methods of setting up a lesson. However, by experimenting with the basic suggestions, you should acquire a working knowledge of some of the materials listed in the book and an added degree of confidence to explore for yourself further possibilities.

Play with the materials. Combine different materials within a composition. Mixing media is no longer frowned upon; most art educators encourage it if it is done purposefully and with good judgment. Have fun; your efforts will be rewarding!

Table of Contents

The Versatile Crayon *(cont.)*

chapter 2
THE WONDERFUL WORLD OF INKS AND DYES   44

A. Techniques Used in Ink and Dye   45

chapter 3
GRAPHICS — REPRODUCE A PICTURE!   57

A. Techniques Used in Graphics   57

The Versatile Crayon *(cont.)*

chapter 6
LET'S EXPERIMENT WITH PASTELS   125

chapter 7
YARN, STRING AND WIRE CREATIONS   134

1

The Versatile Crayon

The crayon — a stick of colored, solid medium, bound together with wax, clay or oil — is probably the most effective and easily controlled medium that can be used in the classroom. It is bright and waxy when applied with a strong and even pressure and, gently applied, it has a light, airy pastel appearance. Its shape produces three distinct surfaces with which to work: the point for detailed sketching; the back for blunt, broad lines; and the side for smooth, large areas (Figure 1-1).

Point- Detail

Back- Blunt

Side - Smooth

Figure 1-1

The crayon has been a much misunderstood tool. For one thing, it is best used if it is unwrapped. The paper binder serves no real purpose, and it hinders the full use of the crayon. Also, broken crayons are not a catastrophe, but an assistance in producing a greater variety of free strokes and shapes.

Because the crayon is so readily available, we often fail to realize how very effective it is. It is clean and easy for all to use; it can be stored and distributed with greater ease than most art media; and the results obtained from its many uses are most satisfying.

Most art educators agree that young children use large, thick crayons because they are easier for them to handle, and areas can be filled in more rapidly. Older children will want to work with the basic stick size that best suits their coordination pattern.

Blending and *shading* colors with crayons produces beautiful results. By laying the crayon on its side and grasping it with the four fingers on one side and thumb on the other side, you can apply pressure at one end of the flat surface and produce appealing, shaded forms. When various colors are overlapped, interesting new colors appear (Figure 1-2).

Figure 1-2

A wonderful, creative lesson can be developed by letting the children experiment with crayon color. They will enjoy discovering how many new colors, shades and tints they can produce from the four or five basic colors they already have.

If a crayon is scratched away or notched along the side with a sharp tool, it can be used to draw a variety of interesting lines and edges. This technique is a good one for older children, and a suggestion from the teacher will spur forth its prompt application (Figure 1-3).

Figure 1-3

The uses and applications of the crayon are limitless. It can be used on different types of materials to produce assorted textures; and it can successfully combine with other media such as dyes, *pastels*, paints, felt-tip markers, inks, pencils and oil crayons for exciting results.

This chapter contains a variety of illustrated ideas that have been planned to familiarize the elementary teacher with the basic understanding of the crayon and techniques in its use.

A. CRAYON ON VARIOUS MATERIALS

We called the crayon versatile, and that is exactly what it is! It can be applied to almost any surface; it is exciting to experiment with to discover how it differs when it is applied and how it appears on different surfaces.

1.Crayon on Paper

Any type of paper takes crayon effectively. Crayon on rough paper will not fill the area as thickly or evenly. However, when using smooth and shiny surfaces, crayons can be rubbed easily and blended into the paper with a rag, ball of cotton or just the fingers.

Manila paper and *newsprint* are probably the most common types of paper used in the classroom. Consider also the use of crayons on

The Versatile Crayon

colored construction paper. The light-colored crayons are most exciting when used on black, brown, gray or any other dark-colored papers. If the colored paper is not available, perhaps manila or newsprint can be painted the shade desired with opaque paint and then colored with crayon.

Other papers that are less often used but are most operative are: cardboard; aluminum foil; oaktag; paper tissues; paper napkins; paper plates; paper doiles; waxed paper; freezer paper; finger-paint paper; *velour paper; rice paper;* sandpaper; plastic wrap; all kinds of wrapping paper; paper bags; and just plain newspaper.

2. Crayons on Textiles

Crayon can easily be applied to textiles. Solid-colored fabric is suggested for most satisfactory results. Also try cloth with a smooth surface or cloth with a strong-woven texture for variety.

Materials: crayons; solid-colored fabric; an iron; newspaper.

* Sketch a design lightly on a piece of discarded sheeting or any solid-colored fabric.
* Rub the color strongly into the area being designed.
* When the drawing is complete, lay the colored area face down on a padding of newspaper and press the back of the cloth with a warm iron.
* Some of the color will melt off into the newspaper; but what remains sets the color into the cloth so it can be hand-washed without losing the basic decoration.

If the crayon has been applied quite heavily, a beautiful print can be transferred from it by pressing the cloth face-down on a piece of manila paper instead of on newspaper when it is ironed (Figure 1-4).

3. Crayon on Wood

Crayon will adhere to any piece of flat-surfaced wood. A piece of *veneer* or driftwood, a tongue depressor, or cedar shingle, a strip of balsa, a piece of discarded crate or fruit box are all adequate for a background.

Materials: crayons; wood; pencil; paper; an iron; felt-tip marker.

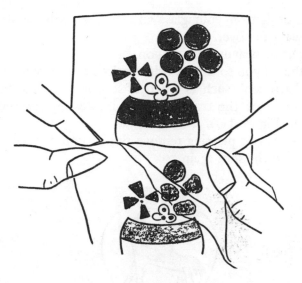

Figure 1-4

* First, draw a subject on the wood with pencil. Then, very carefully fill in the areas with crayon. Use the crayon heavily in all areas to be colored.
* When the picture is complete, lay a piece of paper over it and press it gently with a warm iron. The color will then melt into the wood grain, creating a permanent and very nice *muted* effect.
* The design can remain this way, or it can be given an outline with a felt-tip marker (Figure 1-5).

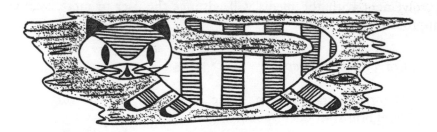

Figure 1-5

4. Crayon on Glass

Materials: crayons; a piece of glass; a mirror; jar or bottle; sharp-pointed tool.

* Draw a design on your glass surface that will suitably fill the area you want to cover.
* Fill the areas heavily with crayon.
* Blend the crayon so that multiple colors can be seen.
* Use a sharp tool, such as a pair of scissors or a nail, and scratch away portions of the crayon for an interesting look at what is underneath (Figure 1-6).
* If an area is not pleasing remove the crayon entirely with your tool, and redo the spot again.

Figure 1-6

B. CRAYON TECHNIQUES USING A MEDLEY OF MEDIA

The following techniques are offered as methods of use, with the crayon as the major material. The author has attempted to list the techniques by the names most familiarly associated with them, although some techniques could also be listed in other categories. It is hoped that the ideas are treated as suggestions, and that further involvement with the media will advance the user to more creative approaches.

1. Crayon on Sandpaper

Materials: crayons; fine-grade sandpaper; paper; turpentine; easel brush; wooden spoon.

* Crayon a picture heavily on fine-grade sandpaper.
* Lay the sandpaper picture aside, and cover the work area with a pad of newspaper.
* With turpentine, coat a sheet of manila paper that is slightly larger than the sandpaper. Use an easel brush for quick strokes.
* Lay the sandpaper over the turpentine-coated paper and, with a

wooden spoon or the side of your hand, rub the back of the sandpaper.

* When the sandpaper is removed, a reproduction of the crayoned picture is left on the coated paper. (Crayon is soluble in turpentine, and a layer of crayon will adhere to the coated paper.) (Figure 1-7.)

* This technique can be repeated several times because the sandpaper texture retains the wax color longer than other types of paper.

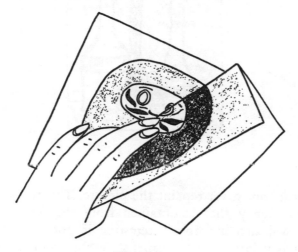

Figure 1-7

2. Crayon Resist

Materials: crayons; paper; tempera paint; easel brush; newspaper.

* Sketch a picture lightly with crayon on a piece of manila paper. Press and fill in heavily those areas that you want to show. Do not cover the entire paper with crayon; allow lots of paper area to show.

* Next, dilute a dark-colored tempera paint about one part paint with two parts water. (The *diluted paint* is often called a *wash* of paint.) Now test the solution on a piece of crayoned scrap paper to make sure the consistency is correct. If the paint is bright and transparent and will roll off the crayoned areas, it is fine. If it is too opaque and covers the crayon, add more water to it.

* Cover the work area with newspaper.

* Place the picture on the newspaper and, starting at the top of the paper with a large easel brush, paint directly over the entire picture. The paint will not adhere to the heavily crayoned areas because the wax in the crayon will resist the water-based paint (Figure 1-8).

Figure 1-8

* One caution: never repaint the picture. This spoils the wonderful transparency that is obtained from the first painting. The picture will also be more interesting if portions of it are not completely painted. Let the paper show through the way it does in a water-color painting.

Variations of Crayon Resist Work

* Colored construction paper makes a wonderful background for crayon resist work. When it is used, it is advisable to use light-colored paint washes over the surface of the crayoned picture for best results.
* Another fascinating variation is to use a crayon that is the same color as the construction paper. When a whitewash is placed over this, it appears as a magic picture.

3. Crayon Tooling

Materials: crayons; paper; newspaper; orange stick or old ballpoint pen.

* Lay a sheet of paper over a thick padding of newspapers, the top layer of which has been thoroughly dampened.

* Press a line decoration into the paper with the dull tool, making a *base-relief* design.

* When the line drawing is complete, dry the paper and fill in areas with crayon.

* Use light crayon in some areas, heavy crayon in others. Try to keep the base-relief designs crisp and free of color (Figure 1-9).

Figure 1-9

4. Crayon Masking

Materials: crayons; paper; masking tape; scissors.

* Construct a complete picture on a piece of paper with bits of cut masking tape.

* Cut the tape narrow in some areas for subjects like a flag pole or thin branch, and use two or more thick strips in areas where wide, broad lines are to be shown.

Figure 1-10

The Versatile Crayon

* Be sure that the tape lies flat and is completely fastened to the background paper. (The tape is being used as a form of line stencil.)
* When the taped picture is complete, cover the entire surface of the paper with crayon. Use striped color or splotchy color all over the paper — tape and all.
* After the crayon has been applied, carefully remove the tape from the picture. The areas covered with tape remain free of color while the other areas of the picture are covered with crayon color (Figure 1-10).

5. Crayon Stencils

Materials: crayons; cardboard or oaktag; scissors; paper; tissues; cotton.

* Cut out an interesting shape from a piece of the heavy paper.
* Carefully cut from the center of the paper so that you can use both pieces as a *stencil.* The one cut out is the positive (Figure 1-11), and the remaining stencil is the negative (Figure 1-12).
* Next, coat the cut edge of both stencils with a heavy layer of crayon.
* Lay your positive stencil on the paper and, using a tissue or ball of cotton, rub the color onto the surface of a piece of background paper. Pull the color from the center of the stencil outward.
* Now use the negative stencil by pulling the color from the stencil into the cut-out area.
* Overlap the designs on the background paper so that your composition is well-balanced and the paper has an all-over pattern on it (Figure 1-13).

Figure 1-11   Figure 1-12

Figure 1-13

6. Crayon-Mock Carbon Paper

Materials: crayons; paper; pencil or ballpoint pen.

* Cover the entire surface of a piece of paper with a thick layer of crayon. Use dark colors for the best results.
* Lay the paper, crayoned side down, on a piece of light background paper.
* With the pencil or ballpoint pen, draw a picture on the back of the crayoned paper. Be sure not to lift up the paper until you have the idea completely on the paper.
* When the top, crayoned paper is removed, crayon lines from it will have formed an interesting picture on the background paper (Figure 1-14).

Figure 1-14

The Versatile Crayon

* Carbon-crayoned paper can be reused for several pictures; just fill in with added crayon the areas of the older pictures where the color has come out.

7. Crayon Encaustic

There are two basic ways that *encaustic* can be used in the classroom. However, each method described must be practiced with considerable care.

a. Crayon Encaustic Using Candle

Materials: crayons; candle; paper.

* Sketch a simple drawing on a piece of paper.
* Light the candle and make sure it is placed at a close proximity and that it is in a firm holder.
* Next, place a crayon tip to the candle flame and, when the crayon is softened, quickly apply it to an area of the picture that was drawn earlier.
* The melted crayon produces dot-like or streaked strokes.
* Continue the process of melting and applying the crayon to the picture until the picture has been completely filled in with thick color (Figure 1-15).

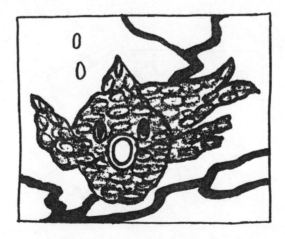

Figure 1-15

* After a bit of experimentation, blending colors while they are still warm produces interesting effects.

b. Crayon Encaustic Using Melted Crayon

Materials: crayon scraps; old muffin tin; a high-voltage bulb that is anchored in a can, or a hotplate (coils not exposed); paper; old brushes; turpentine.

* Sort out the crayons according to color in the sections of the muffin tin. Now place them over the heat to melt.
* Draw a sketch of a simple subject on the paper.
* When the crayons have melted, apply the melted wax color to the areas of the previously drawn picture with a paint brush. Use a different brush for each color. The work must be done quickly, or the wax will harden before it can be applied.
* This technique produces a more vivid color and the texture greatly resembles that of oil paint (Figure 1-16).

Figure 1-16

* Use old brushes and clean them immediately after use with the turpentine.

Variations of Crayon Encaustic

* Crayon Encaustic can be used on paper, wood or cardboard. Try using it on silver foil that has been wrapped around a stiff cardboard shape (Figure 1-17).
* Another interesting technique in this category is Fine-Line Melting. Older children will especially enjoy this. In this process, a piece of paper is crayoned completely with a thick

The Versatile Crayon

coat of wax. Then the blade tip of a wooden-handled knife is dipped into hot water, and while it is still warm, the tip is used to scratch out and melt a design in the crayoned paper.

Figure 1-17

8. *Transparencies*

Materials: crayons; scissors; dull knife or vegetable grater; waxed paper or plastic wrap; an iron; newspaper.

* First, shave the crayons into piles of the same colors on a piece of newspaper.
* Now take two pieces of either the waxed paper or the plastic wrap that are the same size and lay one of them on your working area, placing the other to the side.
* Next, sprinkle the crayon shavings in the areas of the paper to form a picture or design.
* Keep in mind that a few shavings will melt when heat is applied, but color will remain basically the same. The various shavings and combined colors produce wonderfully blended forms.
* Cover the crayon shavings with the remaining piece of paper and place the paper sandwich on a pad of newspaper.
* Now carefully iron the top sheet with a warm iron. If the plastic wrap is used, cover the top of it with lightweight paper before it is ironed. The crayon will immediately melt and *laminate* the paper sandwich together (Figure 1-18).
* The *transparencies* can be left this way or they can be used with other materials, such as cut paper for a framed effect or a

stained-glass window. Portions can be cut and used in a *collage* or in part of a picture.

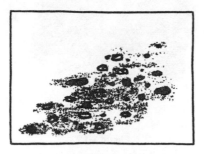

Figure 1-18

Variations

When laminating the paper together with crayon, it will be interesting to add other materials to the middle of the paper sandwich. Cut pieces of construction paper, magazine pictures, string or fabric and place them on the first layer of paper before laminating.

9. Crayon Rubbings

Materials: crayons; paper; string; scissors; miscellaneous items such as doilies, screen netting and sandpaper.

* Place string, cut paper shapes or textured objects such as paper doilies, netting or sandpaper under a piece of lightweight colored or manila paper.
* Feel for the shape with your fingers and, when you have established its location, rub the area with the side of a crayon.
* The raised design underneath will begin to appear on the surface of the paper (Figure 1-19).
* Blend several colors for shaded effects; move the design underneath to another location. *Overlap* and *repeat* the shape. Continue until the entire paper has been designed.

Variation

A wash of water color over the *rubbing* will enhance the rubbing, and you will be combining two techniques: the rubbing with the crayon-resist method.

Figure 1-19

10. Crayon Transfer

Materials: crayons; paper; an iron; newspaper.

A beautiful crayon print can be obtained through a technique called crayon transfer. It is an excellent crayon-graphic treatment that will reproduce the same crayon picture several times.

* Draw a picture on manila paper and heavily color it with crayon. (The legibility of the print will depend on the amount of crayon first applied.)

Figure 1-20

* Lay the picture face down on another piece of paper, which has been placed on a padding of newspaper.
* Press the back of the picture with a moderately hot iron.
* The crayon picture will melt partially into the background surface, forming a print of the original picture (Figure 1-20).

The reproduction is quite pleasing and can be repeated; but naturally, each successive print will be lighter in color.

11. Crayon Marbleizing

Materials: crayons; flat, broad pan; electric hot plate (coils not exposed); paper.

This technique will produce an unusual and exciting result each time. The design is in itself interesting; but portions of it can be cut and used in a collage, mobile or picture.

* Heat water in a flat, broad-surfaced pan.
* When the water is quite hot, drop bits of crayons into it.
* The crayons will melt and the waxy color will float to the surface of the water.
* When this occurs, lay a piece of paper over the surface of the water.
* The crayon, which has been floating on top of the water, will attach itself to the paper.
* Twist the paper to make sure all the color has transferred to the face of the paper.
* Now lay the paper aside.
* The crayon will harden on the surface of the paper and form an interesting, thick, *marbleized* color pattern (Figure 1-21).

Figure 1-21

12. Paper Batik or Bleeding Crayon

Batik is usually associated with the ancient Eastern art of waxing portions of fabric and then applying dye to obtain unique designs. This technique is akin to ancient batik, but uses paper, wax crayons and paint to obtain an unusual effect.

Materials: crayons; brown paper; tempera paint; newspaper; an iron; flat, broad pan.

* First, crayon a design on a piece of brown wrapping paper or an opened bag.
* Use black or brown crayons heavily in a design on the paper, but be sure that lots of paper area remains.
* Next, dip the picture into a flat, broad-surfaced pan filled with water.
* When the picture is saturated with water, take it out and crumple it carefully into a little ball. Now open it up and flatten it on a pad of newspaper.
* Give the flattened paper a wash of diluted, black tempera paint. (One part paint to two parts water.)
* The paint will seep into the cracks of the paper creating an antique appearance (Figure 1-22).

Figure 1-22

* The finished product can dry naturally if a crinkled look is desired, or it can be pressed with a hot iron, face-down, for a flat-surfaced appearance.

13. Crayon Batik on Textiles

Materials: crayons; solid-colored fabric; dye; pan.

* Draw a picture lightly on a piece of fabric.
* Define the drawing heavily with crayon and apply it with strokes that follow the fibers of the cloth. It may be necessary to hold the cloth taut with one hand while this is being done, or the cloth can be tacked to a board.
* If the fabric is of a thin weight, color it with the crayon on the back also, but be careful to fill in areas of color that have already been established on the front of the cloth.
* When the design has been completely filled in with heavy crayon, crumple the fabric carefully into a ball and dip it into the pan of dye.
* The dye will seep into the cracks and penetrate areas of the fabric where the crayon has not covered the cloth.
* Remove the cloth from the dye pan and hang it in a suitable place to dry. (A wire strung across the classroom is an excellent spot.)
* The results obtained from this method will be most rewarding, and a lot easier than the practice used by our Eastern craftsmen (Figure 1-23).

Figure 1-23

14. Blending Crayon

Crayon can be blended in a variety of ways; the following methods are most commonly used.

Materials: crayons; paper; ball of cotton; rags; paint brush; turpentine; eraser.

* On smooth paper, such as finger-paint paper or shelf paper, the crayons can be rubbed with the finger, with cotton or a rag to blend color (Figure 1-24).

* Wax crayon is soluble in turpentine, so if a picture is crayoned with heavy strokes, a wonderful blending can be obtained if the basic design is gone over with a brush that has been dipped in turpentine. The appearance of the picture becomes somewhat blurred and gains the characteristics of having been painted (Figure 1-25).

* A crayoned picture can also be blended by using an eraser to rub one color into another or to rub crayon strokes into smooth areas that look painted (Figure 1-26).

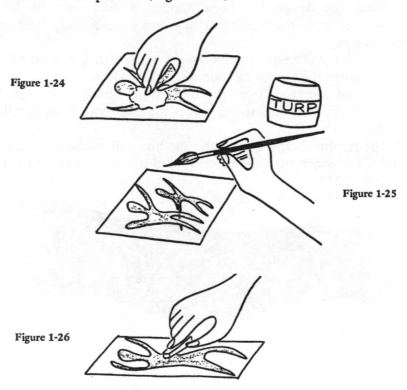

Figure 1-24

Figure 1-25

Figure 1-26

15. Sgraffito or Crayon Etching or Scratchboard

Materials: crayons; paper; sharp pointed tool; newspapers; paper tissues.

* For *sgraffito, crayon etching* or *scratchboard,* first cover the working area with newspaper.

* Then fill a piece of paper with heavy bright colors in any way desired. The color can be put on in stripes, splotchy shapes, or solidly on the paper.
* When the paper is completely covered with bright crayon color, cover the entire paper again, this time with a layer of black crayon.
* If the crayon starts to chip off because of thick application, just apply the crayon in strokes of one direction.
* Occasionally, wipe the area around your work with the paper tissue to pick up the flecks of crayon that come off the paper.
* When the paper is completely covered with black crayon, start to remove portions of the black layer with any pointed tool. (A compass point, a pair of scissors, a nail or an old straight pen are fine to use.)
* Continue to work on the picture until all portions of it have been removed satisfactorily. The design or picture will be more interesting and expressive if the scraping tool is used to make a variety of lines: sharply defined lines and strong, broad lines. The completed work has a fine etched appearance (Figure 1-27).

Figure 1-27

Variations of Sgraffito

* Apply white crayon as the first layer of wax, and black crayon over this. Then scratch through for a black-and-white picture.
* Place light-colored crayons on a piece of paper and overlay this with any other color that will cover it. Scratch through for an interesting and different effect.
* Cover a sheet of paper with a layer of wax crayon. Then, instead of using crayon as a second layer, use black tempera to

The Versatile Crayon

which a few drops of liquid soap have been added. The soap added to the paint permits it to adhere to the waxy-crayoned surface. While the paint is wet, it can be scraped or scratched away with a piece of cardboard, a comb, the handle of a paint brush or a stick. When it is dried, it can also be scratched away with the tools previously mentioned in the other sgraffito work.

16.   *Crayon Glazing*

Crayon *glazing* is another technique that utilizes the crayon with a scraping tool. However, it should not be confused with sgraffito.

   Materials: crayons; paper; dull knife; newspaper; cardboard; scissors.

* Place newspapers on the work area.
* Next, cover a piece of paper with a heavy coat of wax crayon.
* Now cut designs from cardboard and place the shapes under the crayon-coated paper.
* With your fingers, feel for the shapes. When they have been located, take the dull knife and start to scrape away the areas around the shapes. Hold the shapes firmly so they won't move around while working with them.
* Move the shapes and repeat the process. Continue to do this until the scraped designs make an all-over pleasing composition (Figure 1-28).

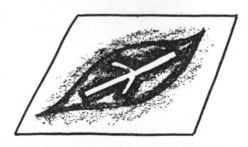

Figure 1-28

17. *Crayon Construction*

The crayon is not only versatile, it is extremely economical because every scrap can be utilized to its fullest degree. Although most crayon work is basically flat in nature, here is a method of utilizing the crayon in a three-dimensional technique.

Materials: crayons; *plasticene;* cardboard or wood block.

* Use tiny bits of plasticene to fasten pieces of crayon together; or fasten crayons together by welding them with wax. (The dripping from a candle is good.)
* Form a firm, thick base with tent formations of connected crayon.
* Build up and out slowly to form a firm, three-dimensional *construction.*
* When the construction has been built to a reasonable height, attach it with the plasticene to a cardboard shape or a block of wood for a base (Figure 1-29).

Figure 1-29

Variation

The construction is quite pleasing as it is in this form; however, wax from a dripping candle can be dropped onto areas of the construction to give it an entirely new appearance.

18. Crayon Sculpting

A very desirable form of *sculpting* can be done by utilizing the wax in crayons with the wax in discarded candles, or, if these are unavailable, pieces of paraffin.

The Versatile Crayon

Materials: crayon scraps; candle stubs or paraffin; large coffee cans; discarded milk cartons; dull knife or nail file; heating element.

* Cut and discard the wicks from the old candle stubs.
* Place the candle pieces or other wax into the can and carefully melt it over a low heat.
* Add crayon pieces for color.
* When the wax is melted, slowly pour the contents into an empty milk carton.
* Allow the wax to harden overnight.
* Peel the paper carton from the wax form, and the shape is ready to sculpt.
* Keep the sculpted work simple. Turn the shape from time to time so that all sides are considered as a part of the whole shape.
* If a portion breaks, heat it slightly with a match flame and return it to its original position.
* Mount the completed shape on a block of wood by heating the bottom of the sculpture long enough for the wax to melt; then adhere it to the mount (Figure 1-30).

Variation

* Use a dull knife to carve jumbo wax crayons into interesting cylindrical shapes (Figure 1-31).

Figure 1-30   Figure 1-31

19. Crayon Mosaics

Tesserae is the tile name for the pieces that make up a *mosaic*. With just a bit of effort, the tesserae can be made of bits and scraps of old crayons.

> Materials: crayon scraps; cans; old cookie sheets; cardboard; rubber cement; heating element.

* Sort crayons of the same color into cans.
* Melt the crayons by placing the cans in a pan of water over the heating element.
* When the crayons melt, pour the hot wax carefully into the cookie-sheet pans.
* While the wax is still warm but not yet hard, cut it into tile shapes.
* Remove the wax tiles when they are hard and repeat the process with new wax.
* Next, sketch a simple design on a piece of cardboard.
* Fill the designed area with the crayon tesserae until it has been completely covered.
* Now, one-by-one, pick up the crayon tiles and attach them to the cardboard with rubber cement to complete the mosaic (Figure 1-32).

Figure 1-32

Variation

Bits of crayon can also be broken or cut into pieces to be used as the tesserae in a crayon mosaic. Try all methods . . .experiment!

2

The Wonderful World
of Inks and Dyes

Inks and *dyes* are not easy media to work with; but they offer wonderful, creative challenges to those who attempt their use. Practice and a good deal of patience are needed before one can master the techniques. However, for all practical purposes, to really enjoy the use of ink or dye one must become acquainted with their many uses.

The ink most often used in art classes for ink drawing is waterproof india ink, which can be purchased under many trade names. It comes both in black and in a range of beautiful colors. There is a shellac binder in waterproof ink so that when it dries, other media can be used over it without smudging or spreading. However, if the teacher feels more confident using washable, non-waterproof ink, she will find that ordinary writing inks are most suitable as a substitute.

There are two types of drawing ink: transparent and opaque. The transparent inks are exquisite in hue but will fade quickly; the opaque inks are used mainly in poster work for lettering. Drawing ink can be applied to paper with pens and nibs in a variety of sizes, or with a brush. Smooth paper of any type is suggested as the best type to use for ink application.

Work space is an important factor in the production of a good ink sketch; and it is suggested that the ink bottle be placed in a safe and stationary position when it is being used. Allow the student to discover through experimentation on scrap paper what kind of lines the pen and brush will make on paper before a project is begun.

Ink used for printing on paper or fabric also comes in tubes or cans of water- and oil-base color. It is suggested that the tube be used in the classroom because of its easier manipulation.

Printing ink is most frequently applied with a *brayer* or *brush.* The water-base printing ink can be cleaned from tools with water; but turpentine must be used to clean the oil-base ink.

Dyes for drawing and printing come in brilliant, liquid hues, and are quite expensive to purchase. However, household dyes in dry and liquid form can be purchased at a considerably lower price and are most suitable for classroom use.

A. TECHNIQUES USED IN INK AND DYE

This chapter will suggest ideas for the use of inks and dyes in a score of new possibilities and approaches that are feasible to use in the classroom.

1. Developmental Ink Scribble

Materials: sheet of smooth paper; pen; nib; india ink.

Figure 2-1

* An excellent device for producing worthwhile experimentation is to divide a sheet of paper (by folding) into squares and rectangles.
* Fill each section with varied ink lines.
* Possibilities may include straight lines, broken lines, curved lines, wiggly lines, crossed lines, and lines put into a series of definite patterns.
* Fill the complete sheet of paper with these experimental exercises until the entire paper has been filled with freehand doodling.
* The paper becomes an interesting sampling of various ink lines and, in the process of developing the page, it becomes an excellent way to acquaint the student with the control of the pen and ink for future use (Figure 2-1).
* Repeat this lesson using a brush instead of a pen in designing each area of paper. The results will be very different.

2. Dry-Brush Picture

Materials: rough-textured paper; large-size brushes; ink.

* Dip the brush into the ink. (Load the brush.) Now wipe most of the ink from it. Use a scrap of paper on the side of the working area to test the amount of ink in the brush.

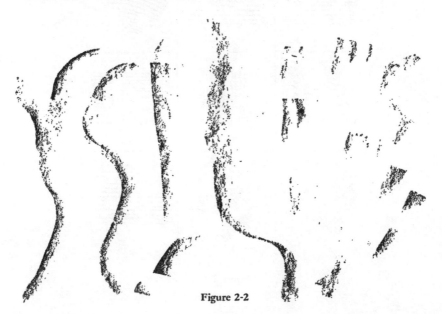

Figure 2-2

* Fan the brush. Do this by laying it open on the paper and drawing it across the paper lightly, adding pressure where needed for more ink.
* The brush strokes produce varying tones of blacks and grays on the paper in flecked dots.
* Take a new sheet of paper and paint a picture with the *dry brush*. See how many tones of black you can get by using the brush in the *dry-brush* method (Figure 2-2).

3. Spatter Print

Materials: smooth paper; scrap paper; scissors; ink; small dish; old toothbrush; stick or tongue depressor.

* Cut some interesting shapes out of the scrap paper.
* Lay them on the smooth paper in a pleasing arrangement. (Do not overlap the pieces, but make sure they are all laying flat.)
* Dip the bristles of the toothbrush into the ink.
* Now hold the brush with the bristle side up, aimed at the cut-out paper arrangement.
* Hold the stick in the other hand at right angles to the bristles and pull back across the bristles away from the paper (Figure 2-3).

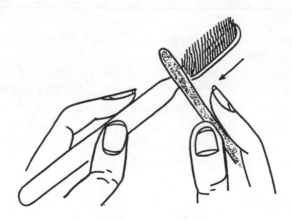

Figure 2-3

* The bristles will snap back and spray flecks of ink on the paper.
* Continue to spray the ink on the paper until the cut-out pieces are covered.

* When the ink has dried, remove the cut-out pieces. You now have a stenciled pattern, in *spatter,* of the shapes you cut out (Figure 2-4).

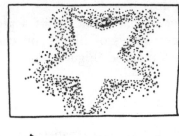

Figure 2-4

Variations

* A variation of the project could be to cut out other stencil patterns and rearrange them over the picture. Repeat the process using colored ink or dye for spattering. The picture now has a multiple set of stencils on it, which overlap in color and create an interesting pattern design.

* Instead of using the toothbrush technique, a spray gun or household atomizer bottle could be loaded with ink and used as the spattering tool. This method is generally used to spray large areas of space. For instance, a snow scene can very successfully be portrayed by spraying the background area with thinned, watered-down white tempera paint.

4. Stipple Pictures

It is not difficult to *stipple* a picture, but it is a technique that can become monotonous.

Stippling is merely dotting the paper with pen or brush-point to form a dotted area.

Materials: paper; pen; brush; ink.

* Draw a picture on paper. Use small pieces of paper at first to experiment with the method.
* Start to stipple-in areas of the picture. The entire composition can be done in stipple of one color or in various colors. If the stippling becomes a chore, combine its use with other techniques.
* Possible combinations might include stippling with crayon, paint or cut-paper work (Figure 2-5).

Figure 2-5

5. Texture Development with Ink

Materials: tube of printing ink; brayer; silver foil; heavyweight cardboard; glue; paper; assorted textured materials such as screen, paper doily, heavily grained wood.

* Glue each textured piece that you choose onto the cardboard for stability. Let them dry throroughly. These become texture plates.
* Squeeze a small portion of the printing ink on the foil and run the brayer through it so that it is coated evenly with ink.
* Now roll the loaded brayer over a texture plate and lay the plate, ink-side down, on paper.
* Rub over it with your hand.
* Lift the plate away and you have a decidedly different type of print (Figure 2-6).
* Try several texture plates.
* An interesting method would be to use the textured prints in drawings or paintings that have been developed. A variety of *textures* can make a *composition* most interesting.

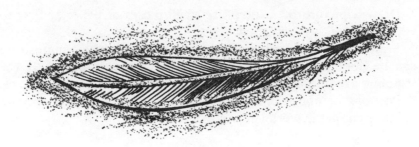

Figure 2-6

6. Ink Batik

Materials: white crayon; brush; ink; paper.

* Cover areas of a piece of paper with the side of a white crayon. Be sure to leave a lot of area free of crayon.
* Now, with brush and ink, paint a picture over the crayoned paper.
* The crayoned areas will resist the ink but the uncrayoned areas will not. The tonal quality of lights and darks in the picture will be exciting (Figure 2-7).

Figure 2-7

7. Ink on Wet Paper

Materials: paper; pen or brush; ink; water; sponge.

* Wet the paper with the sponge in a definite pattern.
* If a large spreading area is desired, saturate the water pattern with more water. If less spreading is desired, let the wet areas dry a little before applying the ink.
* Now draw with the pen or brush on the wet surface.
* The ink will fan and spread into all sorts of unique patterns and shapes. Use less ink on your tool in some areas; in other areas, load the tool with lots of ink.
* Since there is limited control when working in the wet areas, work rapidly.
* When the picture is finished, let it dry; then go over areas again with a pen or brush for highlights that can be captured in the composition (Figure 2-8).

Figure 2-8

8. Scratchboard

Materials: *scratchboard;* ink; brush; scratching tool (old pen nib, large needle, nail, scissors point, or scratch-knife).

Most scratchboard done in the classroom is a form of mock scratchboard (layers of crayon applied to a piece of paper, with the surface scratched to expose crayon color underneath). However, a good teacher should know how scratchboard is done technically; and the correct materials should be used occasionally, even though they are expensive for classroom use.

* Coat the scratchboard (a drawing board coated with an even, chalky top) with black ink.

* Let the inked scratchboard dry thoroughly.
* Now start to scratch out areas with the sharp-pointed tool. A picture is created by scratching white lines out of the black-surfaced board. Work carefully and with little pressure; the chalk coating is easily penetrated.
* Use a variety of cutting patterns in the scratchboard. If a mistake is made, re-ink the portion to be corrected (Figure 2-9).

Figure 2-9

9. Ink and Water Color

Materials: pen; nib; *india ink;* water colors; brush; white paper.

* Draw a simple pen-and-ink sketch on white paper.
* When the ink is thoroughly dried, paint washes of water color over the inked areas.
* If the intensity of the black ink is lost in an area, go over it again with new ink sketching (Figure 2-10).

Variation

* Paint a picture with water color.
* While it is still wet, outline portions of it with pen and ink.
* If you discover that the paint is drying too quickly, redo the painting on fresh paper.
* This time work in picture parts: paint, then ink the portion; paint and again ink the portion until the picture has been entirely completed.

Figure 2-10

10. Blown or Flowing Ink or Dye

There are a number of variations to ink and dye blowing and flowing. A few of the more popular methods will be listed.

Materials: paper; colored ink or dye; cut-up pieces of soda straw; brush; pencil.

a. Straw-Blowing Method

Straw blowing is probably the technique of this sort that can be controlled to a greater degree than the methods that follow later.

* Put a drop of ink or dye on your paper.
* Take a piece of straw and use this for your blowing tool.
* Blow into the straw toward the drop of ink. Continue blowing the ink blob, which runs along the paper in unusual fiber-like finger shapes, until the ink has been used up.
* Put another drop of ink into the basic design already created, or start a new blob away from the one already done. Blow into the straw and create a new ink shape, which can be separate from the first basic shape or blown to overlap the shape already there.
* Continue to add blown shapes until the composition of the blobs has formed an interesting pattern (Figure 2-11).

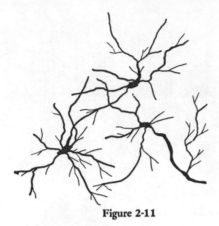

Figure 2-11

b. Blown Ink or Dye

* Place ink or dye drops at random on a piece of paper.
* Now blow or puff at the drops so that they spread out helter-skelter on the paper.
* If a drop dries out, add more color and continue to blow until your desired picture is completed.

c. Ink or Dye Trickle

* At the top of a comparatively long piece of paper, place drops of differently colored dyes or inks.
* Carefully lift the paper from the top and try to control the color drops as they flow down the length of the paper.
* Add drops of color where you would like to extend the flowing process (Figure 2-12a).

d. Flowing Ink Drop

* Draw a simple picture, such as a bird, flower or fish, lightly on a piece of paper with a pencil.
* Now start at any point of the picture by placing a drop of color on the pencil line.
* Then, very carefully and slowly, start to move the paper so that the drop of color moves along the line. This is a quite difficult task; so do not overestimate your ability.
* When the drop of ink runs out, add another drop at this point and continue to manipulate the drop along the pencil lines until the entire lined area has been covered with the flowing ink (Figure 2-12b).

 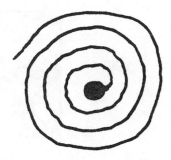

Figure 2-12a   Figure 2-12b

All of the previously mentioned techniques can be combined with other media to produce interesting variations. For instance, the blobs of ink can be blown in a repeated series at the bottom of a sheet of paper to represent the surface of the moon. Space men, done in cut paper, paint or crayon, can be added to complete the picture. Or, a large tree shape can be blown using a straw and india ink. To the large tree shape, a landscape can be added with crayon or paint.

A wonderful *abstract* can also be created out of the flowing ink composition with chalk added to the areas that have not been colored.

11. Fold and Dye Paper

Materials: squares of lightweight paper such as tissue paper or paper toweling; assorted colored dye; flat based pans; newspaper.

* Begin by folding the paper in half and again in half. Then fold again so a right triangle is formed.
* The amount of dye absorbed when the paper is dipped depends upon the length of time the paper fold is left in the dye.
* Now dip the tip-portions of the triangle into one color dye or a variety of different colors.
* Carefully bend the triangle from corner to corner and dip the bent middle section into dye.
* Reopen the triangle and, if there is another area free of color, very carefully dip that portion into dye.
* Open the entire piece of paper very carefully and lay it on newspaper to dry.
* Now take another piece of paper and experiment with the folding and dipping of another design (Figure 2-13).

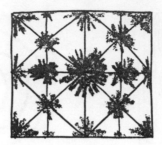

Figure 2-13

12. Symmetry in Ink

Materials: manila paper; ink; brush; newspaper.

* Cover the work area with newspaper.
* Fold the manila paper in half, lengthwise.
* Now open the paper and, on one side of the paper, drop blobs of ink with the brush on the paper.
* Limit the quantity of ink blobs at first.
* Now fold the paper over and press carefully with your hand. (If too much ink was used, it will flood the paper and the design will be lost.)
* Open the paper and look at the *symmetrical design* that has formed. If it is pleasing to the eye, let it remain in this form; otherwise, add other blobs of paint and repeat the process (Figure 2-14).

Figure 2-14

When the symmetrical design is complete, it is a unique form in itself, but it is sometimes interesting to suggest that the children look for something in the design or make something out of the design. In this case, the inked design can be enhanced in composition by adding crayon, craypas or chalk.

3

Graphics—Reproduce a Picture!

Graphics, or printing, as this technique is commonly called, is an ancient and interesting form of reproducing a picture or design.

The processes we use today in graphic art are based on traditional methods that have been altered by experimenting with different materials. Some of the ideas that follow in this chapter are not true graphic art; but in all fairness, they are applicable in our time.

Basically, in graphic work, the surface of a raised or indented material, which is called a "plate," is covered with ink or paint and, when paper or cloth is pressed against it, the design in transferred to it creating a mirror image of the picture on the plate. Often the plate can be used to duplicate the image a multiple number of times. There are a variety of ways to do a graphic and numerous materials and tools that can be used in the process.

This chapter will be devoted to the various ways the teacher can use graphics in the classroom. The collection will provide a fascinating group of ideas that will give the teacher and the students many hours of creative activity. However, the techniques should be used as suggestions, which should lead to other ideas and developments.

A. TECHNIQUES USED IN GRAPHICS

1. Cardboard Prints

Materials: cardboard; scissors; glue; tempera paint; easel brush; paper; pad of newspaper; stiff cardboard for background.

* Use a stiff piece of cardboard about 8″ X 10″ for your background sheet or *plate*.
* Cut cardboard shapes and fasten them to the plate with glue. Continue to cut and glue until you have developed a cardboard picture. Overlapping pieces will make the final print more interesting.
* Set the plate aside on a pad of newspapers and allow the glue to dry thoroughly.
* Now paint the cardboard plate with tempera paint. Do it quickly so that the paint will not dry before you are able to make a print.
* When the surface of the plate is covered with paint, carefully lay a clean sheet of paper over it.
* Rub your hand over the paper, be sure that you press your hand firmly over all areas of the paper.
* Now gently pull the paper away. The paper has pulled a mirror picture of the cardboard plate.
* Repeat the process to create other pictures, and when you find one you like, glue it to a piece of colored construction paper in a contrasting color (Figure 3-1).
* When doing graphic work, sign and number consecutively each print that you pull. This will give the artist a record of the work he has done.

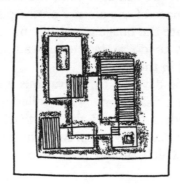

Figure 3-1

2. Inner-Tube Prints

Inner tubes from tires are fairly easy to obtain, and they can be cut so easily with a pair of ordinary scissors that they become an excellent printing medium.

Materials: pieces of inner tube; cardboard; scissors; glue; paper; ink; brayer; pencil; silver foil.

* On a piece of scrap paper, draw simple shapes of a preconceived idea.
* Cut out the shapes and trace them on a piece of inner tube. (Pencil lines will show up remarkably well on the tube.)
* Cut out the inner-tube designs and glue them to the cardboard background (your printing plate).
* Set the plate aside to dry.
* Now put a dab of ink on the foil and run the brayer through it until it is coated with ink.
* Place your plate on a pad of newspaper and roll the inked brayer over it until there is a smooth coating of ink over the entire plate.
* Next, place a piece of clean, dampened paper over the plate and rub it with the palm of your hand until all areas of the paper have been firmly pressed to the plate.
* Carefully pull the paper away from the plate and put it aside to dry (Figure 3-2).

Figure 3-2

* The inner-tube plate is quite sturdy and many prints can be taken from it. Each time you make a print, re-ink the plate.
* Don't forget to number and sign each print. It will add a professional air to the prints.

3. Drip Prints

Here is a technique that requires very little material and yet is a printing method that can easily introduce graphics to boys and girls.

Graphics—Reproduce a Picture!

Materials: tempera paint; paper; pad of newspaper; tongue depressor.

* Lay a sheet of paper on the newspaper pad.
* With the aid of the tongue depressor, drip paint onto the sheet of clean paper. Use a variety of colors, but try to avoid dropping puddles of paint.
* Place a piece of paper over the paint drippings and carefully rub the palm of your hand over the surface of the sheet. Work from the center of the paper outward.
* If paint comes out from the side of the paper, wipe up the excess with a tissue. The newspaper will absorb other excess paint.
* Now gently pull the top sheet of paper away from the original paper plate.
* The print will be an exciting duplication of the dripped paint.
* Continue to take prints of the original until the paint becomes too dry to print.
* Number each print consecutively, and let them dry.
* Choose one of the prints that you consider the best and mount it on a sheet of construction paper (Figure 3-3).

Figure 3-3

4. Collage Prints

Collage prints are fun to make because they utilize all kinds of scrap material. It is interesting to experiment with various materials to discover how many of them can be used to make a print. Allow the children to collect their own material for the collage print. Their homes are wonderful sources for things like bits of lace, doilies, string, sandpaper, textured fabric, paper clips and pieces of old screen

Materials: cardboard of all kinds; scrap materials (those suggested earlier); corrugated paper; printing ink; sheet of silver foil; brayer; pad of newspaper; paper; glue; scissors; *polymer medium.*

* Take a stiff piece of cardboard about 9" X 12" and use this for your background.
* Lay the scrap materials on the cardboard; they must all lay flat in order to print.
* When the arrangement has a nice composition, start to glue the pieces to the cardboard.
* If more than one print is to be made, coat the entire collage with polymer medium for protection.
* Allow the collage to dry thoroughly.
* Now put a dab of ink on the silver foil and run the brayer through it until you have a good layer of ink on it.
* Next, place the collage on the pad of newspaper and roll the brayer over the plate until there is an even coat of ink over the entire surface of the plate. This will be a little difficult at first because of the types and thicknesses of the materials.
* Place the piece of clean paper over the plate and start to rub the area of the paper with the palm of your hand or a wooden spoon.
* Lift the paper away from the plate. The print is an interesting composition of textured lines and shapes (Figure 3-4).

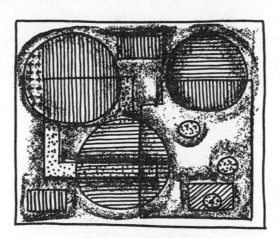

Figure 3-4

* Any number of prints can be taken away from the collage print if the plate has been coated with polymer for protection.

5. Junk Prints

Junk printing is another fun way of doing graphics. The children can collect their own materials for printing. This can be enjoyable because good printing tools must be sought out.

Materials: all kinds of junk material, such as corks; bottle tops; small bottles with wide-mouthed tops; spools; forks; potato masher; cookie cutters; brushes; paper; newspaper; assorted colored tempera paint.

* Cover your working area with newspaper.
* Place a clean sheet of paper over this and begin to experiment with the assortment of junk tools.
* Paint the surface of the printing tool and then press it to the clean paper.
* Use the first paper as a trial sheet and use all of the tools to discover how each one prints.
* Lay the trial sheet aside and then try using the tools that made good prints on a new piece of paper.
* Develop a design by printing with the same tool in columns or in rows. Overlap the printing tool designs; use different colors for variety.
* Continue to make new junk prints, but experiment with different types of paper. Possibly, when the prints are dried, other designs can be added to your prints with crayon or paint and brush (Figure 3-5).

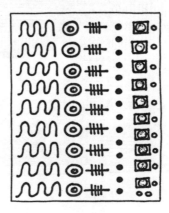

Figure 3-5

6. Rubbings in Crayon or Chalk

A rubbing is probably one of the easiest ways to make a print. Small children will love to use this method because it is fascinating for them to see a design that can be repeated successfully over and over with such little effort.

> Materials: crayon or chalk; lightweight paper; cardboard shapes; lace doilies; leaves; string.

* Place leaves, string, doilies or any textured material under the lightweight paper.
* Find the location of the pieces underneath. Then rub the side of a crayon or piece of chalk over the surface of the paper in the area of the texture.
* You will learn after a bit of experimentation just how much pressure must be executed in order to produce a clearly defined shape.
* Be sure the paper is held firmly while you are rubbing, or else your print will smear.
* Each design will appear on the surface of the paper after it has been rubbed.
* Repeat the process until the paper has a pattern or picture of rubbed designs on it (Figure 3-6).

Figure 3-6

7. Wax Prints

Materials: sheets of paraffin or melted scrap crayons; sharp tool, such as a large pin; old pen; paper; printing ink; piece of silver foil; brayer.

* If old crayons are used, remove the paper wrapping and break them into small pieces. Then melt the crayon bits in an old pot or coffee can. When the wax is melted, pour it slowly into cut-down, waxed milk containers. Allow the wax to harden overnight. Now remove the paper and you have pieces of flat-surfaced wax ready to use.
* With a sharp-pointed tool, draw a line design into the flat-surfaced wax.
* The part cut away will print uncolored; the part not cut will be the color of the ink used.
* Squeeze some ink on the foil and roll your brayer into the ink until it is coated with color.
* Apply a smooth coat of ink over the wax design.
* Next, place a piece of paper that is cut a little larger than the wax block over it.
* Press the paper with the palm of the hand.
* Lift the paper carefully from the plate and place it in a safe spot to dry.
* The wax plate is quite sturdy, and any number of *prints* can be taken from it (Figure 3-7).

Figure 3-7

8. Monoprints

An excellent graphic technique to use successfully with all age levels is a *monoprint.*

> Materials: finger paint; paper; old trays or pieces of heavy cardboard; pencil; combs; sticks; fork.

* Spread a thin layer of finger paint over the back of a tray or over the surface of a heavy piece of cardboard.
* Draw a picture into the painted area with a tool, your finger or fingernail.
* Lay a piece of paper over the painted, inscribed area, and press it with the palm of your hand.
* Remove the paper carefully from the plate and let it dry. You now have a monoprint of the line drawing that was made (Figure 3-8)

Figure 3-8

* Not too many duplications can be made of a monoprint because the paint dries too quickly. When you plan to make many prints of a particular design, keep this in mind.

9. String Prints

> Materials: cardboard; printing ink or paint; sheet of silver foil; brayer; string; glue; paper; newspaper; pencil.

* Draw a simple pencil *sketch* on the cardboard.

* With care, go over the lines of the drawing by squeezing glue a little at a time onto the surface of the cardboard plate.
* As the glue is applied, push string into the glue line.
* Continue to apply the glue and then the string until the lines of the entire picture have been filled with string. Then let the plate dry thoroughly.
* Now place a dab of paint or printing ink on the silver foil.
* Roll the brayer in the color until it is thoroughly coated.
* Next, roll the brayer over the cardboard plate until you have coated it with color.
* Place a piece of dampened paper on the inked plate.
* Press the paper carefully with the palm of your hand. Make sure that the paper is worked down into the string pattern.
* When the paper is removed you will have a beautiful line relief print (Figure 3-9).

Figure 3-9

10. Silk Screen

Silk Screen design is a most important part of the graphic story. There are many forms of this technique, but since we are gearing the ideas to the child and the classroom, I will mention three different techniques than can be used for this purpose.

The "screen" mentioned can be used for all methods outlined.

Materials: water-base ink; finger paint or tempera paint thickened with detergent; a *squeegee*, which can be a tongue depressor, a piece of stiff cardboard used on its side or simply a rubber scraper from the kitchen; the "screen" can be an old embroidery hoop or a cardboard box that has had a hole cut out of it for a frame (any size) with a piece of fabric such as organdy, scrim or thin curtain muslin stretched in it (or taped in the box if that is used); newsprint paper; scissors; newspaper and white muslin.

a. Stencil Method

* Place the fabric in the embroidery hoop or the cardboard frame. Make sure the fabric is taut. This is your screen. Once it is made it can be used interchangably for all methods. The designs can be removed and new ones put on.
* Cut a piece of newsprint slightly larger than the hoop you are using.
* In the center of the paper, cut out a simple stencil design such as a fish, tree or bird. Make sure your stencil cut is not too close to the edge of your paper.
* Place the paper under the hoop or box screen.
* Now put a blob of ink or paint in the fabric opening directly on the cloth.
* With the squeegee, move the paint all over the material right out to the frame of your screen.
* This will make the paper pattern underneath stick to the screen.
* Take away any excess paint and the first print is ready to be pulled.
* Do a few trial prints on newspaper. Place a bit of ink or paint just above the design opening and then carefully pull the

Figure 3-10

printing color over the design, one or two strokes, with the squeegee.

* After the test prints, make several prints on different colored and textured paper. Print the design on a piece of muslin, and make it into something resembling an apron or book cover (Figure 3-10).

b. Crayon Silk-Screen Method

* Make the screen as mentioned previously.
* Now draw directly on the screen with crayon or an old wax candle. The area that is left white is the area that will print.
* Press hard with the drawing tool so that the mesh spaces are filled in with wax.
* Place newspaper under the screen, and then place a blob of color directly on the crayoned cloth.
* Move the paint all over the fabric with the aid of the squeegee.
* A print will appear on the paper underneath when you lift up the screen.
* Many prints can be taken with this method. Experiment with various colors and textures of paper (Figure 3-11).

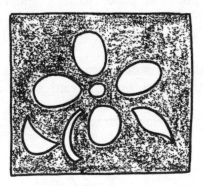

Figure 3-11

c. Silk Screen with Masking Tape

* Make the screen as mentioned previously.
* Cut pieces of tape into different sizes, widths and shapes and fasten them to the bottom of the screen.
* Place newspaper under the screen.
* Put a blob of paint or ink in the opening directly over the fabric. The tape will be underneath.

* Move the paint or ink in the opening directly to the edge of the frame with the squeegee.
* A print will appear on the paper underneath when the screen is lifted (Figure 3-12).

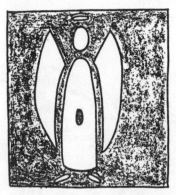

Figure 3-12

* Any number of prints can be made with a masking-tape stencil.

As already mentioned the methods described are for use in the classroom. Professional silk-screen frames can be purchased by the more serious-minded student.

11. Glue Prints

Materials: glue; cardboard; printing ink; brayer; silver foil; paper; polymer medium; brush; newspapers.

* Draw a picture or design on the cardboard by squeezing the glue along the surface to form the lines.
* If you desire a high relief pattern with the glue, let the glue lines dry, and build up heavier lines by applying more glue in the way already described.
* Let the glue dry thoroughly.
* Coating the plate with polymer medium will make it sturdy, and many prints can then be made.
* Now squeeze a little dab of printing ink on the silver foil and run the brayer back and forth until it has a coating of ink on it.
* Roll the brayer over the printing plate. Be sure to cover the surface of the plate completely.

* Next, place a piece of dampened paper over the plate.
* Rub the paper with your hand or the bowl of a wooden spoon until you are sure all parts of the plate have been contacted.
* Carefully pull the paper away from the plate; the print is a line design of the glue drawing.
* Make several prints. Change the color for variety (Figure 3-13).

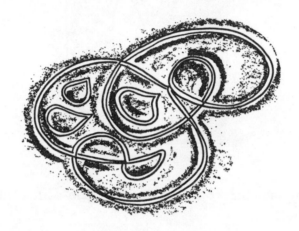

Figure 3-13

12. White-on-White Print

White-on-white printing is a wonderful and different technique. It is really a shallow base-relief done on watercolor paper. The white-on-white creates shadows, which form the basic patterns in the design.

> Materials: inexpensive watercolor paper; heavyweight cardboard; glue; shellac; old metal spoon; large flat tray; water.

* Use a piece of heavyweight cardboard as your backing or "plate."
* To this, glue other pieces of cut cardboard to form a base-relief design.
* When the relief design is suitable, shellac the entire cardboard plate and allow enough drying time.
* Fill the tray with water.
* Now soak the watercolor paper in the large flat tray. Make sure the paper is wet throughout.

* Gently place the wet paper over the shellacked cardboard design.
* Tack the corners down, and begin to slowly rub the wet paper into the relief pattern.
* Use the spoon with care or else the paper will tear, but try to get crisp, clear edges from the design.
* Allow the paper to dry on the cardboard pattern. It may shrink slightly, but this won't interfere with the basic design.
* When the print is dry, mount it on a dark piece of paper.
* The white-on-white shadows create a most interesting piece of work. Try others with deeper base-relief work (Figure 3-14).

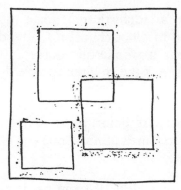

Figure 3-14

13. Sponge Prints

Materials: paint; paper; tongue depressor; flat sponges cut into assorted shapes.

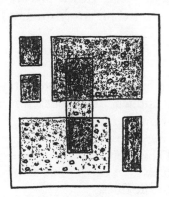

Figure 3-15

Graphics—Reproduce a Picture!

* Using the tongue depressor as a knife, butter the surface of a sponge with paint.
* Lay the painted area of the sponge on paper and press firmly.
* Lift the sponge and continue to print in another spot.
* Butter the sponge whenever it is necessary to do so.
* Change sponge sizes and colors, overlap prints and discover new color combinations (Figure 3-15). Twist and pull the sponge; find new ways to use the sponge tool; try painting a *realistic painting* with a sponge as the printing tool.

14. Celluloid Prints

This technique is a sophisticated form of graphics that is particularly well-suited to older children. Celluoid can be purchased from craft houses, but a wonderful source is the celluloid from greeting-card box tops. Ask the children to save them for the project.

> Materials: celluloid; any sharp pointed tool such as an old pen, large needle or scissors point; printing ink; rags; paper; pencil; sponge; newspapers; small printing press or old washing machine wringer.

* Draw a picture on a piece of scrap paper about 4″ X 6″ with pencil. Keep the picture simple in design.
* Now lay a piece of celluloid the same size over the picture that was drawn.
* Clip the two together so that they will not slide when the work is begun.
* Carefully trace a duplicate of the picture (which is underneath) on the celluloid by scratching away the lines on the surface of the celluloid.
* Scratch lightly at first so that you do not put a hole in your celluloid plate.
* When the picture has been completely traced on the plate, the ink is ready to be applied. Its application is somewhat different from the aforementioned graphic work.
* With a piece of rag, rub some of the printing ink into the lines of the celluloid. (These are the lines that you print.) Keep the surface of the plate as free of the ink as possible. Concentrate on only applying ink to the lines.

* Now dampen a piece of paper by running a wet sponge over it.
* Place the dampened paper over the celluloid plate, and roll it through the wringer or press.
* Test the print for legibility. If more ink is needed, add some. If there isn't enough pressure in your press, pad the plate with layers of newspapers.
* The print is a lovely, fine-line graphic. Many duplications can be made from the one plate. In fact, the plate can be easily washed and put away for future use (Figure 3-16).

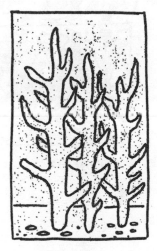

Figure 3-16

15. Heat Prints

Materials: crayons; paper; an iron; pad of newspapers.

* Fold a piece of 12″ X 18″ paper in half, the short way.
* Open the paper and draw a picture in one half of the area of the paper.
* Use the crayon heavily; outline areas that you particularly want to stress.
* When the picture is complete, fold the portion not crayoned over the crayoned area.
* Pad your work area well with newspaper.
* Then heat the iron and press the outside of the folded paper.

* The heat of the iron will melt the crayon and a mirror image of the picture will be transferred in colored wax to the folded, clean half of the paper.
* Display the print and the picture together (Figure 3-17).

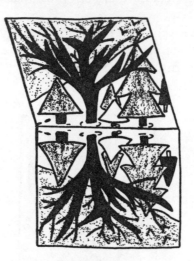

Figure 3-17

4

All About Paint

If one were to take a tally of some sort and ask children what type of art medium they would best like to work with, almost invariably the answer would be "paint." In the realm of the art world, there are any number of exciting art media, but the liquid freedom and vibrant color that paint renders makes it most desirable to the child.

Paint, according to Webster, is "a mixture of a pigment with some suitable liquid to form a solid adherent covering when spread on a surface in thin coats for decoration." There are a variety of paints that are offered to the child-artist. In the classroom, the suggested types include tempera or poster paint, water colors, finger paints and the newer plastic or acrylic paints; and the use of all should be encouraged. *Oil paint*, needless to say, is not functional for elementary-class use.

Tempera or *poster paint* has a heavy quality. It is *opaque* in nature, and covers a painted area. It comes in two forms: liquid and powder. The latter must be mixed with a suitable liquid. Excluding the usual water, other possibilities are milk, liquid starch and liquid soap.

Watercolor has a light quality and is *transparent* in nature. It comes mainly in cake form and must be mixed with water. The use of watercolor leaves a film of beautiful, see-through color on the surface of the paper.

Finger paint has a thick quality and comes in liquid and powder form. The powder must be mixed with water or liquid starch.

When commercial fingerpaint is not available, liquid tempera can be mixed with liquid starch, and this makes quite an adequate substitute. Because the hands and arms are the primary painting tools in finger painting, most children like working in this medium.

The plastic or acrylic paint is the newest type of paint to be used in the classroom. It has marvelous qualities, which make it most versatile. It comes both in bottles and in tube form. If it is used with a little water, it is opaque, similar to tempera paint. If lots of water is used with it, it becomes similar to watercolor in transparency. If it is built up layer upon layer, and polymer medium is used with it, it then resembles oil paint in appearance.

The polymer medium can also be used as a glue and, if it is used to cover *acrylics,* it renders a shiny surface to the area covered. A great advantage in using acrylic paints is that they dry very quickly, can be worked over when completed, and are waterproof when dry. Gesso is often used with the acrylics. It is a white plastic paint that can cover almost any type of surface and thus make it ready for the use of acrylic paint. However, it does not necessarily need to be used. Acrylics can be applied directly to paper, cardboard, wood or other surfaces.

One disadvantage of acrylics is that one must remember to constantly keep the brushes in water when they are not being used. The rapidity of the drying quality of the acrylics makes the brushes useless if they are not washed thoroughly after use.

Not too much is needed to set the stage in motion for painting. A good working area, brushes (if possible, a large, 1-inch stiff-bristle brush and one pointed camel's hair brush for each child), paint and a container of water are the essential materials to begin with. Add to this a smock for the more cautious, newspapers to cover work areas and a paint cloth for clean-ups.

Try some of the following techniques; they will open doors to endless possibilities in the realm of painting in the "Art World."

A. HOW PAINT CAN BE USED

1. Crackled Paper

Materials: shiny paper such as finger-paint paper or shelf paper; tempera paint; large, hard, 1″ bristled brush; pointed camel's hair brush; pan of water.

* Wet the paper. This can be done by holding it under running tap water or by rubbing it with a wet sponge.
* Slowly fold and crumple the sheet of paper into a ball.
* Open it carefully and lay it on the work area, which has previously been covered with newspaper.

* Now, using the large brush, cover the paper completely with tempera paint. Notice how the paint runs into the cracks and forms dark line patterns.
* When the paper is covered with paint, lay it aside to dry.
* Next, using the pointed brush, define in black paint some of the patterns made with the cracks of paper.
* If a crackled area seems to represent something, fill it in with other colors to complete the picture (Figure 4-1).

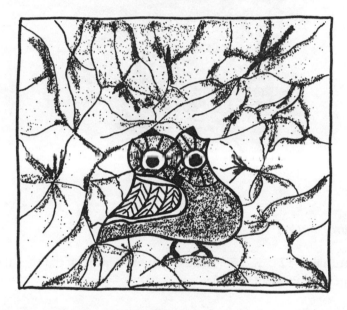

Figure 4-1

2. Paint-and-Crayon Antique

Materials: tempera paint; brush; water; crayons; 12″ X 18″ manila paper; hot tap water.

* Paint a picture using tempera paint.
* Allow the picture to dry and then go over each painted area with a layer of *contrasting*-colored crayon.
* Be sure that the crayon is put on quite heavily.
* Now hold the picture under hot running water.
* The hot water will melt the crayon and bits of it will be washed away.
* When the picture takes on an antiqued appearance, set it aside on a flat surface to dry (Figure 4-2).

Figure 4-2

3. Swirl Painting

Materials: 12″ X 18″ manila paper; tempera paint; salad oil; large cookie sheet; water.

* Fill the cookie sheet partially with water.
* Mix separate containers of tempera paint, each with about one teaspoonful of oil.
* Pour the colored mixtures on the surface of the water. With the handle of a paint brush, swirl the paint slightly. Do not mix, or else the colors will *neutralize* and not be crisp.
* Now lay the paper over the swirled paint.
* Allow the paper to float on the surface of the paint and water mixture for a second or two; then carefully lift it away.
* The design, which has transferred to the paper, will resemble colored marble.
* To repeat, add more paint-oil mixture, and you will be able to make other designs.
* You will discover that no two picture designs will be the same. This technique is accidental but extremely interesting and fun to do (Figure 4-3).

Figure 4-3

4. Paint Rubbing

Materials: cardboard shapes in different thicknesses; finger paint; shiny paper such as finger-paint or shelving paper; heavy 3″ X 6″ piece of cardboard, or a food scraper to be used as a squeegee.

* Lay the cardboard shapes under the piece of shiny paper. Tape the corners so the paper will not move.
* Cover the entire area of the paper with a thick coating of finger paint. (Your hand is the tool).
* Now pull the food scraper up and down the surface of the paper. As this is done, the paint is removed in areas and the cardboard shapes underneath are slowly defined in deeper color.

Figure 4-4

All About Paint

* Set the picture aside; rearrange the pieces and lay a clean sheet of paper over them.
* Now repeat the process with another color.
* If you choose to do so, other materials such as plastic doilies, string, heavy sandpaper, etc., can be used for other textures (Figure 4-4).

5. Mingling

Materials: 12″ X 18″ white paper; sponge; water; watercolors; brush; newspaper.

* Cover the work area with newspaper.
* Wet the surface of a piece of paper thoroughly with the sponge and water.
* Now, while the paper is quite wet, drop blobs of watery paint on it with the brush.
* Use different colors and watch the paint float from puddle to puddle, creating a beautiful and exciting mingling effect.
* When the composition of color is satisfactory, set it aside to dry.
* The mingled-paint picture can remain as it is, or a fine brush can be used to define a representational picture over the mingling, which may accidentally appeal to the imagination (Figure 4-5).

Figure 4-5

Variation

A variation of wet paint and wet paper can be made, which is most effective and is somewhat controlled.

* Wet a piece of paper and paint directly on it without any preliminary sketching or drawing.
* The picture will remain representational and yet have a fresh sparkle of accidental color and blending.
* The technique is most exciting to try and the results will change if various types of absorbent paper are used.
* Try a piece of rice paper for an extra treat.

6. Sponge Painting

Materials: assorted colored tempera paint; sponges of all sorts, cut or torn into a variety of sizes and shapes; manila paper, 12" X 18" in size.

* Dip a sponge into paint and make some large, free shapes on paper.
* When you see what one piece of sponge will do, try other pieces.
* Pull, twist, smear, dot or dab the sponge.
* Try using it flat or use the sharp edge on the side.
* Add other colors and mix what you have already applied.
* When one picture has been completed, try another using a realistic idea. The sponge is the tool; use it as a brush (Figure 4-6).

Figure 4-6

All About Paint

7. Painting on Cloth

Materials: a piece of closely woven, solid-colored fabric; tempera paint; liquid starch; stiff-bristled brushes; newspaper; tape; an iron.

* Cover the working area with a pad of newspaper.
* Tape a piece of fabric to the newspaper. This will hold it relatively taut.
* Make a thick paste of a variety of different colors of tempera, which has been mixed with liquid starch.
* Paint the picture or design using the paint mixture. Put the paint on heavily so it will seep through the fibers of the fabric.
* Let the picture dry thoroughly and then press the fabric face-down on a pad of newspaper.
* The painting makes a unique wall hanging. Stitch across the top, slide a dowel through, and your painted fabric is ready to display (Figure 4-7).

Figure 4-7

8. Spray Painting

Materials: diluted tempera paint; commercial spray gun or any refillable spray container; manila paper; cut paper shapes or found objects such as leaves, buttons, twigs, fern or string; newspaper.

* Fill the spray can with watered-down tempera paint. Test the consistency so that the spray is even and the paint does not clog the spray hole.
* Next, cover the work area with newspaper.
* Now lay the found objects or the cut paper shapes on the manila paper. The shapes will act as a stencil.
* Hold the spray container a short distance from your prepared composition and begin to spray the entire composition. The stencils as well as the paper will be covered with color.
* Allow the paint to dry, and then remove the stencils.
* The color arrangement can be changed by relocating the stencil shapes to other parts of the composition and spraying again. Change the colors; you will find exciting things happening with the blended color.

Variation

Spraying can be done in a large cardboard box, which is placed on an elevated height such as a table. The spraying is then confined to the inside of the box. When you use this method, however, the stencils must be pinned or taped slightly to the paper, and then the paper must be pinned to the back of the box before spraying. This type of spraying is excellent because it minimizes the clean-up after the spraying is completed (Figure 4-8).

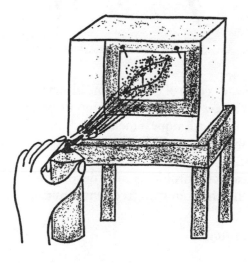

Figure 4-8

All About Paint

9. Blow and Trickle Painting

Materials: diluted tempera paint; white or manila paper; brush; soda straws; newspaper.

* Cover the work area with newspaper.
* Place blobs of watered-down tempera on the paper.
* Experiment first by holding the paper at an angle and allowing the paint to flow freely in one direction; then turn the paper to another angle and change the direction of the paint trickle. Continue to do this until the paint is dissipated.
* Now try putting blobs of paint on the paper; and just blow or puff at the blob. In this case, your paint will fan out into interesting tree-like shapes (Figure 4-9).

Figure 4-9

* Another, more controlled way of blowing paint is to blow through a soda straw to disperse the blob of paint.
* Use all of the techniques mentioned or try each technique singly in a composition. This method is a very unusual way to design with paint.
* Caution: Headache problems may develop if too much blowing is done. Have the children stop frequently during the lesson.

10. Imagination Blots

Materials: 12″ X 18″ white paper; water colors; brush; newspaper.

* Cover the work area with newspaper.

* Fold the paper in half, the long way, and reopen it so it is laying flat on the newspaper.

* Now, along one half of the paper, put blobs of paint. Be sure the blobs are not puddles.

* Next, refold the clean side over the paint blob and rub the top of the paper several times with your hand.

* Open the paper and you will find a beautiful symmetrical design on the paper.

* Now turn the paper in different positions and use your imagination to aid you in discovering possible realistic objects you see in the blot. It may be a butterfly, an insect, a little animal. In this case, use a tipped brush and other paint to make the picture more representational. Crayons, pastels, paint and brush can be used to develop the idea that has been formulated (Figure 4-10). Experiment!

Figure 4-10

11. Tape Painting

Masking is the technique we are exercising when we do a tape painting. The knowledge of this method will lead to other creative efforts that will be found very rewarding.

Materials: manila paper; tempera paint; brush; masking tape; scissors.

* Work directly on the paper without any preliminary sketching.

* Start by cutting a few pieces of tape into different lengths and thicknesses.

* Place the pieces of tape on the paper just as if you were setting

All About Paint

up a drawing. You will find very shortly that the tape becomes your pencil or brush.

* Continue cutting and placing the tape until the entire idea you have planned is executed on the paper.

* The tape must lie flat so that there are no little "air pockets."

* When the entire picture has been drawn with the tape, run your hand over the entire surface of the paper to be sure the tape is all flat.

* Now cover the entire paper, tape included, with paint. How it is applied does not matter. It can be covered solidly with one color or painted in stripes or patches of color.

* Let the paint dry; then carefully remove and discard the pieces of tape.

* The picture is composed of the white, protected parts, which were under the tape.

* Additional painting or crayoning can be done on the picture but keep the white, masked areas bold and crisp (Figure 4-11).

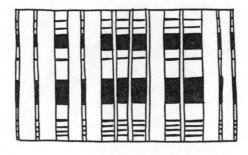

Figure 4-11

12. Point Painting

A famous artist from the French School named Georges Seurat originated a type of painting called *Pointillism.* This is simply painting a complete picture with tiny dots or points of color. Here we have a modified form of this method, which can easily be done with the point of a brush or a Q-Tip (cotton swab).

Materials: tempera paint; pointed brush or Q-Tips; jar lids; paper; pencil.

* When making the first pointillist picture, keep the idea simple and work on a piece of paper about 9" X 12" in size. This method

takes time, and the first composition should not be too ambitious.
* Put a small quantity of paint in each jar lid so that there is a variety of color to work with. One Q-Tip will also be needed for each color.
* Dip the cotton tip into the paint and start to fill in those portions of the sketch that you have already drawn.
* It is a good idea to outline the various lines you have drawn with the color you want the area to be. In this way, you can fill in the spaces thus outlined with color.
* Do not put the dots too close to one another; you may want to add other colors in-between to form new colors, the way Seurat did.
* When the picture is completely finished in point form, mount it on a piece of dark paper (Figure 4-12). This will accentuate the pointillist method.

Figure 4-12

Variation

Try emulating Van Gogh's technique: Paint a picture using swirled or streaked lines with paint, the way the artist did in his painting "The Starry Night."

13. Cardboard Painting

The title of this section implies that you use cardboard as a material to paint on. It is true that this can be done, and most effectively if you use corrugated paper. The paint seeps into the grooves of the cardboard and becomes mingled, to form other colors.

Try this idea for a new "canvas" material; it can really spark up a lesson (Figure 4-13).

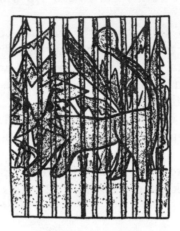

Figure 4-13

However, let me suggest another technique that uses cardboard as a tool for painting.

Materials: cardboard of all types and thicknesses cut into a variety of sizes; tempera paint; jar lids; manila paper; newspaper.

* Cover the area with newspaper.
* Put a variety of paint colors into the jar lids.
* Place the manila paper on the newspapers and have the cut pieces of cardboard available.
* Dip the edge of the cardboard into the paint and begin to paint a picture using the lines formed by pressing the paint-dipped cardboard edge onto the paper.
* Use different-size pieces to make different-size lines.
* Cut the painting edge into teeth or curves for a swirled effect on paper.
* Pull the cardboard edge down the paper when you want to fill in an area solidly.
* Wipe the cardboard on the newspaper when you want to use the same size in another color paint. If the cardboard becomes too limp, discard it and cut a new piece.
* When the picture is completely painted, lay it aside to dry and

try another picture, experimenting with the cardboard in other
ways (Figure 4-14)

Figure 4-14

14. Vaseline Prints

This technique could also be categorized as a form of graphics, and
rightly so, because it is a printing process. As a matter of choice,
however, the author chooses to place it among the paint techniques.

> Materials: petroleum jelly (Vaseline); powder paint or thick
> tempera; mixing container; manila paper, 12″ X 18″; news-
> paper; pencil.

* Spread newspaper over the working area.
* Mix the paint with petroleum jelly until it is a thick-colored
mass.
* Cover a piece of manila paper with the jelly mixture. Use your
hand as the tool and make sure that the jelly is applied in a thin,
smooth layer.
* Next, place a piece of clean paper over the colored mixture.
You now have a paper sandwich with colored petroleum jelly
inside.
* Keep the paper pieces together.
* Quickly draw a picture on the top of the paper sandwich. Work
freely and fill in areas by just running the pencil back and forth in

those areas. Do not press too heavily with the pencil point or else the paper will rip.

* Gently pull the paper sandwich apart. You will find two prints: a positive and a negative.

* Lay the two prints aside to dry. You will find that they dry quite quickly.

* When the technique is familiar, intricate prints can be made using this method (Figure 4-15).

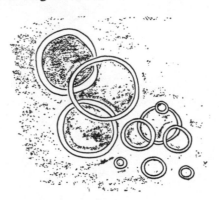

Figure 4-15

15. Paint with Unusual Materials

When a child paints a picture he is basically interested in putting down a pictorial idea. Although the medium and the tools are important, they are basically secondary in his thought. The painting act is his artistic creativity and not the picture he produces.

Here are a few painting materials that can be most intriguing. They are experimental and should be used as such. Have fun!

KOOL AID: Mix different colors of this food drink and use them for the color. Use large pieces of manila paper and large brushes for the painting (Figure 4-16).

TOOTHPASTE: Mix the toothpaste with powdered paint to form a thick paste. Work on a piece of cardboard and use a tongue depressor as the spatula tool to paint a big bold abstract (Figure 4-17).

FOOD COLORING: Use the food coloring undiluted, directly from the bottle. Work on smaller pieces of manila paper using

Figure 4-16

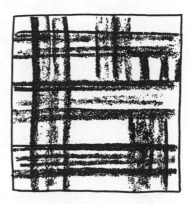

Figure 4-17

fine-pointed brushes. Try the pointillist method with this medium. Unique hues develop from the use of this color.

FLOWER PETALS: Use any form of the flower when it is wilted, but not when it is dry. Gather the petal up in a little ball and either pounce it on the paper with a dabbing motion or rub it into the paper. It is best to work in a small area, and have a preliminary sketch made to fill in with the colored juice of the flower petal. Experiment with all types of flowers. Notice how the color of a petal does not necessarily become that color when it is applied to the paper. Use leaves and pieces of bark and make other discoveries with nature's colors (Figure 4-18).

Figure 4-18

All About Paint

16. Antiquing with Paint and India Ink

Materials: tempera paint; heavyweight 12″ X 18″ paper; brushes; India ink; newspaper; running tap water.

* Cover the work area with newspaper.
* Paint a picture using the tempera paint. Use the paint quite heavily. Allow some areas of the paper to show.
* When the paint is dry, go over the entire picture surface with India ink.
* Again, let the paper dry.
* Now hold the picture under running water and begin to wash away the ink.
* The length of time the picture remains under the running water determines how much toning effect will be obtained.
* Experiment with several pictures in order to produce the *antiquing* effect you most desire (Figure 4-19).

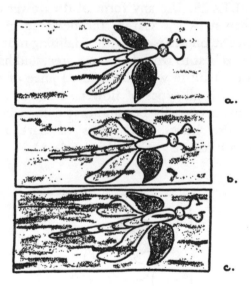

Figure 4-19

17. Painting with Felt-Tip Markers

The felt-tip marker is a comparatively new item in the art world. It is used quite extensively in the classroom because it is considered by many to be less "messy" to use than paint. One must remember that although this is a consideration, paint is a fluid, free, spontaneous liquid, which can combine colors to make new colors and can be used in tones of lights and darks. These characteristics make paint a unique material.

Materials: felt-tip markers in a spectrum of colors; paper.

* When using the markers in a classroom, the teacher must allow each child the complete freedom in choosing colors. The student must not be inhibited by the choice of a scant variety of color offerings.
* Painting with markers can be done without a preliminary sketch; or the sketch can be drawn lightly before the application of the marker color.
* Complete areas should be filled in with color, but the markers must be used with a light hand. Too much pressure will produce blobs of color in undesired areas.
* Use the marker in line design combined with other materials, such as crayon or chalk; or paint a complete picture filling in all areas with color from the markers (Figure 4-20).

Figure 4-20

18. Still-Life Painting

Here is an interesting way to have an art lesson. Some art educators frown on this practice because they say it does not allow the child true creative expression. However, occasionally a copy of some form of representational art is excellent practice for the child-artist.

Materials: tempera paints in a variety of different colors; 12" X 18" manila paper; brushes; newspaper; paint rag;

* Set up a still-life composition. This can be an interesting task. A bouquet of flowers, bowl of fruit, driftwood pieces, shells, almost any creative arrangement will be satisfactory for the study.
* If the classroom is large, arrange several compositions so the children can choose the one they would like to portray.
* Suggest that an outline of the composition chosen is drawn on the paper with diluted orange paint. This can be covered or reworked.
* When the outline is completed, further developments can be made with other colors.
* State that the picture, although representational in nature, does not have to appear that way, sketch or color-wise. The artist has the right to change the composition and color scheme to suit his own prerogatives.
* Children enjoy doing a still-life paintings and they should have the opportunity to do them, but with the abundance of art possibilities, use this one sparingly (Figure 4-21).

Figure 4-21

19. Paint Outdoors with Watercolors

Materials: watercolor box; sponge; brushes; water container; white paper; newspaper; watercolor pad.

* If the painting is done outdoors, find a spot where the materials can be used comfortably. Work with the pad propped up on a

makeshift easel or lean it on your knees. If you are working indoors, work in an area next to a window so the scene you portray can be observed readily. Cover your work area with newspaper and place the materials in a usable position.

* When working with watercolors, it is a good idea to cover the large areas, such as the ground, the sky, and water, before anything is filled in with detail.

* First, dampen the surface of the paper with water. You can do this with the brush or, more quickly, with the sponge.

* Then use a "wash," which is a little paint and lots of water.

* Assuming that the sky is done first, load a big brush with the wash. Start at a top corner and make a stroke across the paper to the edge; slide the brush down; go the opposite direction to the other edge. Then repeat the process until your wash has been completely used up.

* If you are not successful in loading your brush sufficiently, it may be necessary to load the brush again and start the color at the point you left off.

* Avoid going over the wash. Watercolor is transparent and should stay crisp. Going over what you have done will make the colors "muddy" or give the appearance of ribbons or stripes across the paper.

Figure 4-22

* When the sky is complete, turn the picture around and do a wash for the ground or water the same way you did the sky. If the paper needs rewetting, do so before you start your wash.
* When the ground and sky are done, let the paper dry.
* Now add other things you might like to include in your picture with a pointed brush loaded with lots of paint and very little water. The details that complete your picture should cover the light wash areas underneath (Figure 4-22).

20. Paint with Acrylics

Materials: a piece of cardboard; aluminum pie tin; tubes of acrylic paints; brushes; *gesso;* container with water; newspaper; polymer medium.

* Cover the work area with newspaper.
* Coat the piece of cardboard with the gesso; it will give a better painting surface to work on.
* While the gesso is drying, squeeze a variety of color from the tubes of paint in a spectrum of color. The aluminum tin makes a good *palette* for thinning or mixing the paint.
* Experiment with the paint. You will find that by using a lot of water with it the paint will react as does watercolor. Using it as it comes from the tube will give the appearance, when built up in

Figure 4-23

layers, of oil paint. If polymer medium is used with the paint, it becomes shiny when dry.

* Keep the brush in water when not in use.

* Experiment by first making a splotchy-colored abstract on the cardboard background.

* When the picture is complete, go over it with gesso. This will cover what you have done and you will have a fresh working area to work on.

* Now that you have experimented with acrylics, begin a new picture and, this time, plan precisely how you want to use the material (Figure 4-23).

21. Sandpaper and Paint

Materials: 9″ X 12″ cardboard; sandpaper; glue; brushes; liquid; tempera paint; pencil.

* Coat the cardboard with a thin layer of glue. Wash out your brush.

* Now make a preliminary sketch on the cardboard with a pencil.

* Start to fill in areas of the picture with tempera paint. It will be necessary to apply several coats of paint in each area.

* Allow the paint to dry thoroughly when the picture is complete.

* Now begin to sand away portions of the picture until you can see the portions of the cardboard underneath.

* The picture can be worked to any point that is desirable to the artist. The work should take on an antiqued appearance (Figure 4-24).

Figure 4-24

All About Paint

5

Paper Capers Are Fun!

Paper construction work is one of the most rewarding art media in which to work. If boys and girls are exposed to basic paper techniques and are allowed the freedom to investigate and discover with various types of paper, their reponse is very enthusiastic and fruitful.

Before encouraging the use of paper in construction work, the child must first learn some of its possibilities. The knowledge of building basic forms and how to complete a project with finesse are important elements to be learned. Basic techniques such as cutting freehand geometric shapes with scissors, constructing cones and cylinders, fringing, pleating and curling paper are invaluable exercises. Once the manipulation of these techniques is learned, the imagination will act as a springboard from which creative paper construction will be a result.

Little is needed to work successfully in paper construction. Scissors, rulers, rubber cement or a suitable adhesive, tape, staple machine, staples, and, of course, paper are the basics. It is a good idea for the teacher to keep a box of assorted cut, colored and textured paper somewhere in the classroom for easy accessibility. The students can then experiment with the paper to make discoveries and develop solutions that will be their own individual creation.

A. CHANGE THE SHAPE

It is amazing to discover the number of possibilities that exist when working with a piece of paper. I always think of the trick that involves a 12″ square of solid paper, which you are asked to walk through. Of course, this is an impossibility; but with a pair of scissors and some hearty cuts the paper becomes expanded to such a degree that an adult can literally walk through it. Paper cutting can be magic!

Section A of this chapter involves knowledge of the basic techniques used in paper construction. Section B deals with suggested activities using the techniques first mentioned and ideas for using various types of paper. These possibilities are offered, but it is hoped that the information given will open new doors to the creative use of paper and three-dimensional paper work.

The materials needed for the following exercises are so similar that they will be listed at the beginning of this section.

> Materials: paper in a variety of weights and sizes; scissors; clips; tape; stapler; rubber cement.

1. Paper Curls

* With the exception of very heavy paper, all paper can be curled to some degree. A loose curl can be made by simply wrapping a strip of paper around your finger, while a tighter curl can be made by wrapping a pencil into a paper strip (Figure 5-1a).

* The more agile person can hold a strip of paper in one hand and, with a scissor blade in the other hand, pull strips of the paper across the cutting edge of the scissors, which will make the paper curl (Figure 5-1b).

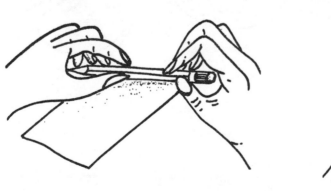

Figure 5-1a   Figure 5-1b

Paper Capers Are Fun!

* Any way used to curl paper will create a three-dimensional effect, which will add interest to a paper product.

2. Curl-a-ques

* Making a curl-a-que is another way of expanding paper.
* Take a circle of paper or cut one out by folding a square of paper three times and cutting it at the loose end in an arc (Figure 5-2).
* Then start at one point at the outside of the circle and continue to cut around and around until the middle is reached (Figure 5-3).
* If the curl-a-que is large and long it will make a wonderful moving spiral. If it is small and fat its center can be pulled out and tacked to make another type of three-dimensional shape (Figure 5-4).

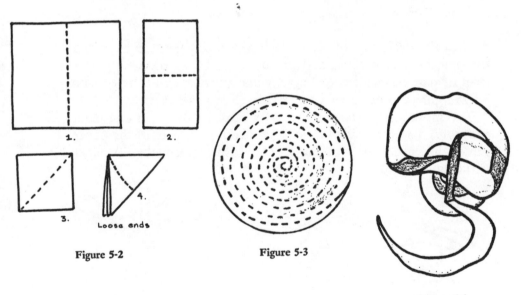

Figure 5-2   Figure 5-3

Figure 5-4

3. Fringe

* To fringe is simply to cut a piece of paper in a repeated uniform cut. The width of the slit is entirely up to the cutter.
* The fringe cuts can be thick or thin, long or short. No matter what the method, you are changing a flat-surfaced paper into an interesting pattern form (Figure 5-5).

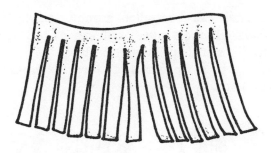

Figure 5-5

4. Pleating

* Pleating is an attractive and easy way to change the shape of a piece of paper. It is often called a fan or accordian fold because it resembles these shapes when completed.
* Start with a rectangular-shaped piece of paper.
* Fold it the short way about 1″ in width.
* Use the thumbnail to go over the fold so the crease is firmly established.
* Next turn the folded paper over so the folded portion is face-down on your surface.
* Again fold the paper so that the fold underneath is exposed.
* Continue folding in this manner until the entire paper has been used in the pleating.
* The pleating can be held together at the bottom with a staple, tape or clip (Figure 5-6a).

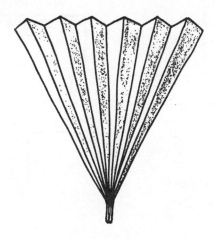

Figure 5-6a

Paper Capers Are Fun!

* The two ends can be pulled around and fastened to form another circular-pleated shape, or it can be left open and pulled around to form a star shape (Figure 5-6b).
* The folds can be snipped away to form yet another lacy-shaped form (Figure 5-6c).

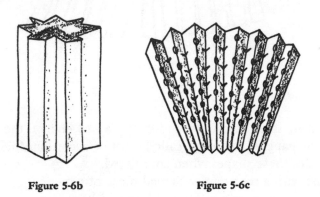

Figure 5-6b   Figure 5-6c

5. Cat Stairs

* Cat stairs are made by taking two long, narrow strips of paper and pasting or stapling them together in an L formation.
* When this is done, a series of folds is made. A is folded over B, B is then folded over A, and this is continued until the strip is completely folded into a small square (Figure 5-7).

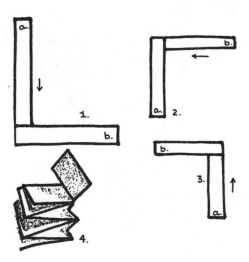

Figure 5-7

* At this point, the end flaps are pasted together and the cat stairs are completed and ready to be used as a part of a construction.

6. Cones

* A cone is a wonderful three-dimensional stand-up shape. It is made by flapping the straight edge of half a circle (B and C) around into a cone shape and fastening it securely (Figure 5-8).
* The rounded edge becomes the base of the cone.
* This shape has many potential uses, the main one being the base for a beginning construction.

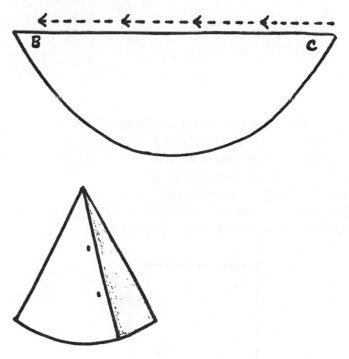

Figure 5-8

7. Cylinders

* A cylinder is a rectangular piece of paper of any size, which has two short ends (A and B) flapping one over the other to form a closed round space (Figure 5-9).
* It is a pleasing shape to use as the base of a project, or it can be used to strengthen other three-dimensional shapes.

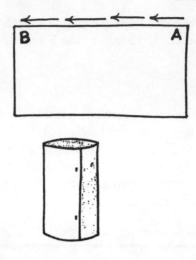

Figure 5-9

8. Pyramids

* A pyramid is another stand-up shape, which is exciting to use when working with large three-dimensional shapes.
* It is formed by folding a square of paper diagonally 2 times — corner to corner — A to B, and C to D.
* Next, cut along the fold D to E.
* Flap and paste triangle F over triangle G and the shape becomes a most impressive paper pyramid (Figure 5-10).

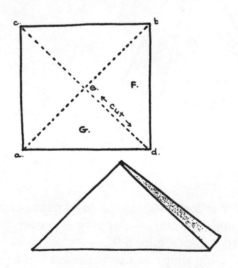

Figure 5-10

9. Scoring

* *Scoring* a piece of paper is literally making a scratched stroke or line on the paper with a tool such as the blade of a pair of scissors, a nail-file point or a dull knife point. This can be done freehand or with the aid of a ruler.
* With a scored line you are actually making a fold in the paper in a shape that a fold cannot make.
* The beauty of a scored-line fold depends upon the quality of the paper. Experimentation with various types of paper will best indicate those paper types that are better for individual use (Figure 5-11).

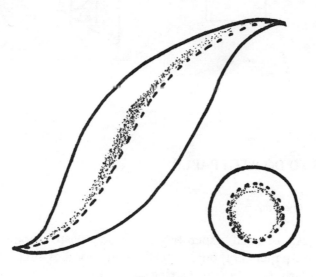

Figure 5-11

10. Slit Magic

* An interesting way to attach heavy paper or cardboard together is by taking two pieces of paper, each having cuts made in them from the bottom to the center of the paper.
* Be sure that the cuts are straight cuts.
* Slip the slit of one piece of paper into the slit of the other.
* The two pieces interlock to form a sturdy fastening.
* The possibilities with this technique are endless, and only experimentation with it will prove how far you can go (Figure 5-12).

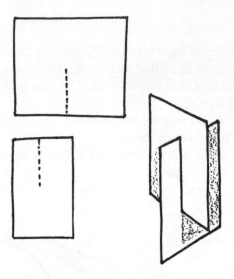

Figure 5-12

B. THINGS TO DO WITH PAPER

1. The Lowly Bag

Materials: assorted paper bags; scissors; paste; scraps of construction paper; crayons; miscellaneous goodies such as bits of tissue, yarn, lace, buttons, string and fabric.

a. Puppets

* A wonderful puppet can be made using a square-bottomed bag as a base. The face is made on the rectangular section of the bottom of the bag.
* The puppet is manipulated by placing the hand in the open end and moving the fingers at the top of the bag to make the flap move up and down.
* The movement emulates a talking puppet (Figure 5-13a).
* When the face of the puppet is completed, decorate the bottom section of the bag with cut paper or any of the suggested materials to make the puppet into any character desired (Figure 5-13b).

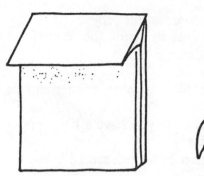

Figure 5-13a   **Figure 5-13b**

b. Puppets with Finger Openings

* Srill another bag puppet can be made by cutting a hole in the center of a small paper bag.
* The hole becomes the nose of the puppet.
* Decorate the area around the nose with cut paper or other goodies to complete the face of the puppet.
* Curl some paper strips and add them to the top of the bag for a new kind of hair (Figure 5-14).

Figure 5-14

Paper Capers Are Fun!

c. Paper-Bag Piñata

* Use a large bag from the food store for this project.
* Stuff it with crumpled newspaper and the traditional Mexican contents — candy, fruit, little gifts.
* Next, tie the top securely.
* Now take another smaller bag, fill it with newspaper and tie the top.
* Fasten the two bag tops together so you have a body and a head for your animal or bird piñata.
* For a bird piñata, add wings that have been scored in curved lines; add pleated legs for a bouncy look.
* Cut and shape a small paper cone for his beak.
* Curl strips of paper for a bushy tail (Figure 5-15).
* An animal puppet is made by the addition of legs and ears instead of wings and beak (Figure 5-16).

Figure 5-15   Figure 5-16

d. Bag City

* Make an entire city out of houses and buildings that are made of bags.
* Follow the basic idea for this house, and then make several others using different structure plans each time.
* Puff out a bag so the rectangular bottom will stand up when it is placed on a flat surface.
* If the bag seems too high for the house or building, cut the top of the bag until the size is satisfactory.
* Next, carefully refold the bag to its flat shape and, with

crayons or paint, draw the windows, doors, the siding material on the building, a porch, flower boxes, or any other pertinent structure that will identify the building you are trying to create.

* Do both the back and front of the buildings.

* If the side of the bag is opened carefully, that portion of the bag can also be colored.

* Reopen the bag and glue it to a cardboard base.

* Now stuff the bag with some crumpled newspaper to give it some stability.

* Take a 4" X 6" piece of construction paper and fold this in half the short way. Carefully place it on top of the opened bag. This is the roof of the building. If it seems too large, trim it with scissors wherever necessary.

* Tack the roof to the building with a bit of glue; add a chimney with cut paper.

* After completing one building, continue with other bag constructions until an entire city has been made (Figure 5-17).

Figure 5-17

e. The Bag as a Surface for Doing Art Work

* A paper bag cut into squares and rectangles makes wonderful pieces of paper on which to draw or paint.

* The brown paper takes on a completely different texture and working surface if it is treated in the following manner.

* Crumple a piece of brown paper bag into a tight ball.

* When there are many wrinkles in the ball, open it carefully and smooth it out so it can be drawn upon.

* The wrinkled paper takes on the appearance of bark or leather.

* It is excellent to use as simulated bark for a Mexican Bark Painting; or it can be used as a leather skin on which to draw Indian designs with crayon or felt-tip markers (Figure 5-18).

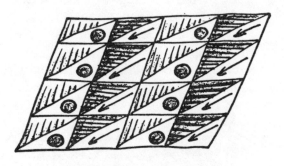

Figure 5-18

2. Corrugated Cut-Outs

Materials: corrugated cardboard about 9" X 12" in size; scissors; pencil; paint.

* Draw a simple, large sketch on the corrugated paper.
* Define the sketch with heavy pencil.

Figure 5-19

* Next, use the pointed, sharp edge of the scissors to incise the pencil line. Do it carefully so the point doesn't slip and cut anything but the top surface of the corrugated board.
* As the surface is cut, slowly pull off the pieces that separate from the board (Figure 5-19).
* Continue removing portions of the surface paper so the cut-out work forms an interesting, textured pattern.
* The project can be painted or left in its natural state.

3. Cylinder People

Materials: white paper 12" X 18"; rubber cement; scissors; assorted-colored construction paper; stapler.

* All kinds of people, animals and birds can be made with cylinder shapes.
* Bend a piece of white paper around to form a cylinder.
* Fasten it in this shape by pasting or stapling the cylinder closed.
* Decide what the cylinder shape will be.
* Concentrate on the facial features. Cut out the paper eyes, ears, nose, and mouth and fasten them to the cylinder.
* When the face is completed, add the arms and feet.
* Curl paper for hair.
* Add a paper cone for the hat or an umbrella for some character.
* Complete with cut-paper scarf, belt, collar, etc. (Figure 5-20).

Figure 5-20

4. Torn-Paper Art

Materials: assorted-colored construction paper; 12″ X 18″ manila paper; rubber cement; crayons.

* Experiment with the tearing of paper. Try tearing with the forefinger and thumb of your two hands close together, and the paper can be controlled to a greater degree.
* Tear a face, nose, hair and other body shapes.
* When you feel competent at tearing a specific shape, such as the subjects already mentioned, attempt tearing a shape such as a house, car, animal or human figure.
* Now choose the shapes that you feel you were successful in tearing, and paste them to a piece of manila paper in an interesting composition.
* When this is done, unify the torn paper shapes by adding a crayon background to the picture (Figure 5-21).

Figure 5-21

5. Cardboard Faces

Materials: cardboard in a variety of thicknesses; scissors; rubber cement; tempera paint; brushes; 12″ X 18″ cardboard background; pencil.

* Sketch a face depicting an animal, bird or person on the background cardboard with pencil.
* Now begin cutting the cardboard pieces in shapes depicting the various features of the sketch.
* Pyramid the cardboard pieces in layers, one smaller than the

other, until thicknesses are built up. This will add a three-dimensional aspect to the drawing.

* Continue to build up each individual section until the entire face has a compilation of three-dimensional features.
* Attach the layered cardboard features with rubber cement.
* Now paint the areas of the face for added interest (Figure 5-22).

Figure 5-22

6. Picture Puzzles

Materials: a sheet of sturdy cardboard at least 9" X 12"; compass; tempera paint; brushes; scissors.

* With the compass, draw the largest circle possible on the sheet of cardboard.
* When this is complete, cut it out and then lightly sketch a picture on the circle.
* Paint the picture with tempera paint. Use the color freely to make the picture stand out boldly.
* Allow the paint to dry thoroughly; then cut the cardboard circle into a variety of shapes and sizes. Try to keep the pieces comparatively large in size.
* The new home-crafted puzzle will give a great deal of satisfaction to its creator for a long time (Figure 5-23).

Figure 5-23

7. Crepe-Paper Painting

Materials: crepe paper in assorted colors; scissors; 12" X 18" white paper; water; bucket; sponge.

* Cut pieces of crepe paper to make a picture.
* Use the manila paper as the background and, as the cutting is done, lay the pieces on it so you can plan for future cutting.
* When all the pieces are cut and the picture appears satisfying, carefully lift off the cut shapes and lay them carefully aside, using the same picture plan as you did before.
* Now wet the background paper thoroughly with the sponge.
* Quickly return the cut shapes to the wet paper, placing them in their proper original position.
* Another piece of wet white paper can be placed on top of this to form a paper sandwich with the crepe paper in between.
* Now rub the top of the paper carefully with the side of your hand. Carefully remove the top piece of the paper and the pieces of wilted crepe paper.
* How exciting it is to discover that the dye has seeped out of the crepe paper and has penetrated the two pieces of white paper.
* The result is a duplicate print, painted quite mysteriously with dye from crepe paper (Figure 5-24).

8. Build a Giant

Materials: assorted-colored construction paper 12" X 18" in size; scissors; paper cement; 9" X 12" manila or flesh-colored paper.

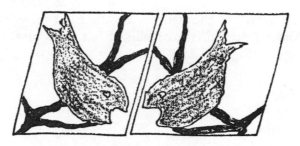

Figure 5-24

* Round off the corners of a 9" X 12" sheet of manila or flesh-colored paper for the head of the giant. Add a small rectangle at the bottom for a neck of the same color.
* Take the 12" X 18" paper, whatever color desired, and make the upper half of the giant.
* If the paper is held the long way it will elongate the size; if it is held the short way, the figure can be made stocky.
* Keep adding paper to build up the body. The torso can be made any size, and it is fun to exaggerate the size of the body by the addition of paper.
* When the body is the size desired, cut the 12" X 18" paper in half the long way and start fastening the legs and arms of the figure.
* Again, make the legs and arms as long as desired to stress the size of the giant.
* When the legs and arms are long enough, attach hands and feet.

Figure 5-25

Paper Capers Are Fun!

* Now add details to the figure with other cut paper and rubber cement. Make a cat-stair tie, a cylinder hat and a pleated scarf for the grand giant (Figure 5-25).

9. *Tissue Fun*

a. Acrylics with Tissue

Materials: assorted-colored tissue paper; polymer medium; brush; water; 12″ X 18″ white paper.

* Tear pieces of tissue into smaller pieces and slowly plan a picture using the colored tissue. (It isn't necessary to have a planned picture beforehand; it is fun to just experiment with the materials as you work.)
* If placement of the color is unsatisfactory, omit the tissue, or add tissue to areas to be reinforced.
* When the picture plan is acceptable, begin covering the tissue with polymer medium. Do this by applying it like paint with a brush. Apply the polymer, a small quantity at a time, working on one piece of tissue at a time. (Note that the polymer is used in an entirely different manner from other adhesives when using the tissue. It is used over the tissue, not under it.)
* Continue adding the polymer until all the tissue has been adhered to the background paper.
* Some color will come off the tissue, but this will only add interest to the composition.
* Remember to always keep the polymer brush in water when it is not in use, and always wash the brush immediately after completing a picture.

NOTE: Tissue pictures can also be made by fastening the tissue to the paper with other adhesives used under the tissue. However, the glazed finish that the polymer adds to a tissue-polymer picture is most desirable (Figure 5-26).

b. Crumpled-Tissue Pictures

Materials: tissue in assorted colors; white paste; 9″ X 12″ manila paper; pencil.

* Plan a simple sketch of a picture on the manila paper. Keep the shapes large.

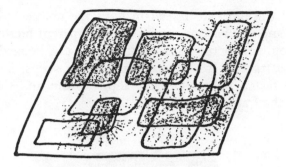

Figure 5-26

* Now tear the tissue into small pieces, crumple them into a small ball, and start to fill in the areas of the picture with the crumpled-tissue balls.
* If the paste is applied to the paper in small areas, and the tissue is placed into the paste, the picture will take on a neater appearance.
* Continue adding the paste and tissue until the entire picture has been filled in with tissue-paper color (Figure 5-27).

Figure 5-27

10. Cellophane with Felt-Tip Marker

Materials: cellophane; 9″ X 12″ manila paper; pencil; scissors; felt-tip marker; black paper; rubber cement.

* Pencil sketch a scene on a piece of manila paper.
* Now cut a piece of cellophane the same size as the manila paper and lay it carefully over the sketch.
* Using the felt-tip marker, go over the lines that were made in the pencil sketch directly on the cellophane.

* When all the lines are traced in with the marker, pick up the cellophane and you have an interesting transparent picture.

* The cellophane picture is quite fragile. It can be made stronger and more attractive if you cut black paper strips, about 2" in width, and fasten them along the top, bottom and sides of the picture for the frame (Figure 5-28).

Figure 5-28

11. Newspaper Art

Materials: newspaper (preferably the sheets printed with want-ads or stock quotations); paint; crayon; pastels.

Newspaper is one of the most easily obtainable and yet most forgotten art materials. It is invaluable as a liner under art work for quick clean-up afterwards; and the newspaper itself is excellent to use as a background when working with paint, crayon or pastels. True, the print shows through these materials, but this heightens the interest created in the picture.

Here is an idea using a combination of two materials in an exciting technique.

* Cut the newspaper into a large rectangle.

* With pencil, draw a rectangle within the rectangular-shaped paper. (A 2" border around the penciled rectangle would be fine.)

* Now, with the side of a pastel, put blocks of color in the penciled rectangle. Use at least three colors of pastel, and vary the patches of color so the rectangle, when completed, will resemble a patchwork quilt.

* When the color is all blocked in, decide upon a simple drawing such as the sketch of a boat scene, birds, fishes, flowers, vegetables, which can be drawn heavily over the pastel with a black crayon.

* The picture is quite handsome when completed.

* Now try the same sketch used in the pastel-crayon picture on another piece of newspaper. This time paint the scene. The newsprint under the pastel-crayon really lends an interesting aspect to the picture, doesn't it? (Figure 5-29).

Figure 5-29

12. Crazy Quilt (Wallpaper)

Don't neglect to accumulate wallpaper whenever possible. It can be used in a main project or to supplement another project. Try this idea; you will find it most interesting.

Materials: 12″ X 18″ manila paper; assorted pieces of wallpaper; thick, black yarn; rubber cement; scissors.

* Cut wallpaper pieces into shapes and carefully fit them onto the manila paper into patterns resembling a crazy quilt.

* Paste the pieces to the manila paper.

Figure 5-30

* When the paper is completely covered with the wallpaper shapes, take the thick yarn and start to define areas around the shapes with the yarn. Cut and paste the yarn around each of the shapes until each piece of wallpaper in the entire picture has been outlined. The completed picture is most impressive, and you have a new way to use up excess wallpaper (Figure 5-30).

13. Cardboard Construction

Refer to Part A, Number 10 in this chapter, Slit Magic, which deals with a unique way to attach paper together with the aid of cut slits.

Materials: oaktag or light-weight cardboard; scissors.

* A simple free-form shape is the best way to start working with slit construction. For this, cut the cardboard or oaktag into a supply of rectangles of all sizes and shapes.
* Now cut slits in the shapes from the bottom to fit the middle, but make sure the slits are straight and not on a slant.
* Next, start to lock one rectangle slit into the slit of another.
* The shapes can have multiple slits cut into them so you can attach the pieces to the side and build out as well as up.
* Continue to add the shapes until the construction is built up to a pleasing free-form shape.

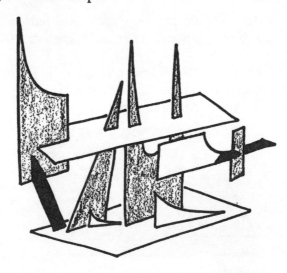

Figure 5-31

* The construction will remain intact as is, but it can be reinforced with a dab of rubber cement at each slit for more permanence, if needed (Figure 5-31).

14. Paper Masks

There are any number of ways to make a mask. Here is a way that is a bit different, and one that will always produce an outstanding project.

Materials: 12" X 18" oaktag; scissors; stapler; paint; brushes; assorted cut paper; rubber cement.

* Take a piece of oaktag 12" X 18" in size and fold the bottom end up about ¼ of the way (Figure 5-32a).
* Next, take the folded corners (A and B) and fold them up to the edge of fold C, and staple to the fold (Figure 5-32b).
* Now cut away the portion of this area in a half-circle to make a comfortable spot in which to place the chin (Figure 5-32c).
* Put the mask over your face and, with a pencil, carefully place a dot on the outside of the mask at the location of the eyes, nose and mouth. Remove the mask.

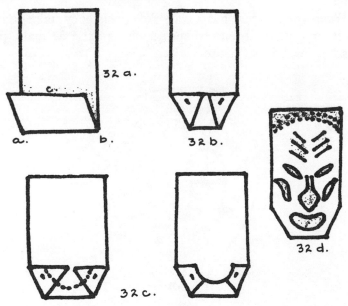

Figure 5-32

* Next, stab the scissors through the dots depicting the placement of the features, and cut these areas out.
* The mask is ready to be decorated with paint and cut paper (Figure 5-32d).

15. Papier Mache

One of the most outstanding types of art techniques is the art of *papier mache.* The children like to do it, and there are three distinct ways to work with it. Basically, the work involves just the use of paper and watered-down paste. The three methods — pulp, strip and sandwich mache — are given in detail here:

Materials: newspaper; wallpaper or white paste; paint; brushes; polymer medium.

a. Pulp Method

* Make a mixture of torn pieces of newspaper, wallpaper paste and water in a large container.
* Let the mixture remain overnight, and if the mixture appears too thick, add more water. If it appears too thin, add more torn paper.
* When the mixture has a clay-like consistency, take quantities of it and mold it into shapes such as little animals, puppet heads, pins, beads (Figure 5-33).

Figure 5-33

* Allow the pieces to dry for several days and then paint and coat with polymer medium.

* If beads are made mold them around a knitting needle or stiff wire so the hole is formed while drying.

SUGGESTION: Add a few drops of oil of cloves to the papier mache mixture if it is not used immediately. It will halt spoilage and the odor that goes with it.

b. Strip Method

* When you work in the strip method with papier mache, what you are doing is using a base such as a bottle, balloon, electric bulb, can or box as a form to cover with strips of paper and paste. The end product is a strong and sturdy construction.

* Tear paper into strips about 1″ wide and 6″ long.

* Make a mixture of two parts paste, one part water in a bowl.

* Now cover one side of a strip with paste and place it on the form. Suggest that the strips lay flat, like adhesive tape.

* Continue to do this until four or five layers of strips have been put on the shape. Alternate the strip position so that one layer is put on vertically and the next is put on horizontally. Make sure when applying the strips that they slightly lap over the strip before, so there are no spaces in between.

* Allow the shape to dry overnight. Then paint and coat it with polymer medium to complete the project (Figure 5-34).

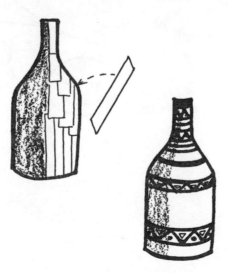

Figure 5-34

c. Sandwich Mache

* Sandwich four or five layers of manila paper with undiluted white paste in this fashion:

* Coat a piece of manila paper with paste.

* Cover it with another sheet of paper, and again coat the paper with paste and cover it with paper.

* Continue this process until you have a five-layered paper sandwich with four layers of paste between.

* The paper sandwich is most pliable and easy to handle.

* Cut it into a shape, and turn up the sides to make a bowl; or lay the paper sandwich over a turned-over bowl and shape it to the bowl sides (Figure 5-35a).

* Cut off the excess paper at the bottom.

* Use the excess paper to cut out shapes for pins or any other small objects.

* Let the shapes dry overnight, and then paint them with tempera paint. When the paint dries, coat them with polymer medium or shellac. Glue a pin back to the small objects so they can be worn (Figure 5-35b).

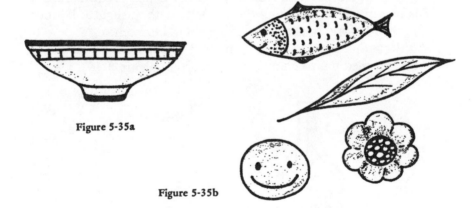

Figure 5-35a

Figure 5-35b

6

Let's Experiment with Pastels

A pastel is a powdery chalk stick made of ground and mixed pigment, chalk, water and gum. When used by itself, it has a soft, delicate hue and a light, subtle tint. The pastel is most often used simply to draw with, as you would with crayon. However, the nature of the material, if you allow experimentation, lends itself to many interesting art experiences.

A. USEFUL HINTS AND TECHNIQUES

Most people shy away from the use of pastels because they say they are a messy medium in which to work. They are messy to work with, it is true, but there are a number of things that can be done to alleviate the clean-up created by the use of pastels.

One way to help the user of pastels is to first cover the working area with an ample supply of newspaper. Then, when a project is completed, the newspaper can be folded carefully and discarded, with all the pastel residue inside. Another helpful suggestion is to work with a moistened towel available. Then, when hands need to be cleaned after the use of a pastel, this can be accomplished by simply wiping the fingers with the wet towel.

One more suggestion can be made to facilitate easy manipulation of pastels, that is, to pick up a picture at intervals and drop the excess chalk-powder onto the newspaper above the working area, or to carefully carry the picture to the waste-barrel, where the chalk-dust can be shaken from it. This is far better than blowing the chalk-dust off the picture onto the floor, as so often occurs.

The suggestions given may be criticized by some as hindering the creative process. However, it must be remembered that creativity does not mean unorganized messiness. Creating a meaningful, worthwhile project takes thought and planning.

Now, let's try some of the great possibilities that exist in the use of this medium — pastels.

1. Casein Pastels

Materials: 12" X 18" colored construction paper; newspaper; pastels; sponge; a container of any one of the following: milk; powdered milk; buttermilk; sour cream.

* When working with *casein* pastels, first cover the work area with newspaper.
* Place the colored paper on the work area.
* Saturate the surface of the colored paper with the sponge and the milk product chosen.
* Now draw on the surface of the milk-laden paper with the pastel in any fashion you care to express.
* Use your fingers, nails and the side of the hand to push the pastel color around the paper, just as if you were working with finger paint.
* When the picture is completed to your satisfaction, put it carefully aside to dry (Figure 6-1).

Figure 6-1

2. Crackled Paper and Pastels

Materials: 12" X 18" white, shiny paper (finger-paint paper or shelf paper would be fine); scrap pieces of pastel; newspaper; liquid starch; small pieces of sandpaper; black paint; brushes.

* Cover the work area with ample newspaper.
* Crumple the piece of white paper into a tight wad; then carefully open it up and lay the crackled paper on the newspaper.
* Now cover the entire sheet of crackled paper with a layer of liquid starch. This can easily be done by brushing it on or by pouring a small portion on the paper and spreading it with the hand.
* Next, quickly take the scrap pieces of pastel and begin to rub them on the sandpaper to form colored powder.
* Let the pastel powder drop directly on the shiny, white paper so it forms patches of color in the liquid starch.
* When there is enough colored powder on the paper, spread the color into the cracks of the paper with the hand.
* Allow the crackled paper to dry. Then define areas of the paper with black paint and brush for an interesting composition (Figure 6-2).

Figure 6-2

3. Powdered Pastel Stencils

Materials: scissors; heavyweight paper; 12″ X 18″ manila paper; pastels; wad of cotton; newspapers; *fixative* or hair spray.

* First cover the work area with newspaper.
* Cut a stencil with the heavyweight paper. A free-form shape is a good shape to use (Figure 6-3a).
* Now place the stencil on the manila paper. Carefully apply the pastel in heavy layers around the edge of the stencil.

* Rub the pastel color from the edge of the stencil to the surface of the manila paper with the aid of the cotton wad.
* If more color is needed, apply more pastel powder to the stencil and repeat the rubbing from the stencil to the paper.
* Move the stencil whenever you choose to do so. Repeat the stencil pattern in another area; overlap for interesting results.
* When the stenciled picture is complete, spray it with the fixative or hair spray (Figure 6-3b).

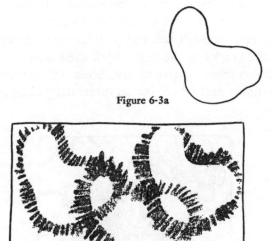

Figure 6-3a

Figure 6-3b

4. Pastel Rubbings

Materials: 12″ X 18″ manila paper; pastels; scissors; heavyweight paper.

* Cover the work area with newspaper.
* Now cut the heavyweight paper into a variety of interesting shapes and sizes.
* Then, carefully place them under the manila paper.
* Next, carefully rub the side of a soft pastel over the entire manila-paper covering.
* The shapes underneath will become visible on the surface of the manila paper.

* Lift the covering and move the shapes to new areas. Now replace the paper covering to its original position.

* Change the pastel color and again make a rubbing, this time of the new arrangement. The results will be a rubbing transfixed over the first rubbing. The overlapping will give depth and new excitement to the composition (Figure 6-4).

Figure 6-4

5. Pastel String Design

Materials: string; 12" X 18" manila or white paper; tape; pastels; scissors; newspaper.

* Cover the work area with newspaper.

* Place the manila paper on the work area and then cut the string in pieces the length and width of the paper.

* Above the work area, lay the string on the newspaper and run the pastel stick over the string many times, so that the string will be coated with chalk color.

* Then fasten the string taut with the tape from one side of the manila paper to the other (Figure 6-5a).

* Now lift up the center of the string and let it snap back on the paper.

* The chalk string will leave a line of color on the paper.

* Change the chalk color on the string and attach it to another position on the manila paper.

* Again snap it by lifting the center and letting it go.

* Continue to change the position of the colored string until there is a network of colored lines on the manila paper (Figure 6-5b).

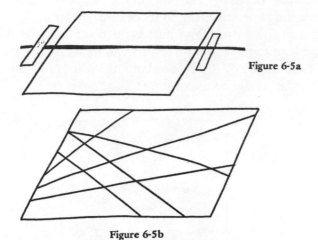

Figure 6-5a

Figure 6-5b

6. Pastel on Sandpaper

Materials: A sheet of rough sandpaper; pastels; newspaper; pencil; fixative or hair spray.

Pastels are usually delicate and light in color tone. However, when used on sandpaper the color becomes vivid and bold.

* Cover the work area with newspaper.
* Lightly sketch a pre-planned idea on the sandpaper with pencil.
* Now carefully fill in the areas sketched with pastel color.
* When complete, spray the picture with fixative in order to preserve it (Figure 6-6).

Figure 6-6

7. Wet Paper and Pastel

Materials: 12″ X 18″ manila paper; container of water; sponge; newspaper; scrap pastels; fixative.

* Cover the work area with newspaper.
* Put the pastel scraps into the container of water.
* Saturate the manila paper with the sponge and water.
* Now rub the wet pastels onto the wet paper.
* Use your fingers and hand to pull the color around the paper.
* Make a bold abstract with the wet chalk. Outline areas of the composition with dark-colored pastels.
* Lay the picture aside to dry.
* When dry, spray with fixative (Figure 6-7).

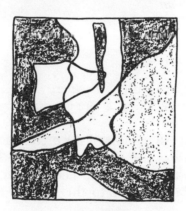

Figure 6-7

8. Pastels on Dark Paper

Materials: 12″ X 18″ dark-colored construction paper; pastels; newspaper; cup of liquid starch; pencil.

* Cover the work area with newspaper.
* Lightly sketch a picture on the dark-colored construction paper.
* Fill in some areas with dry pastels.
* Dip the chalk in the liquid starch and apply this to areas of the picture.
* The use of the combined dry and wet pastels creates a textural

effect on the dark paper, which used in itself with dry pastel almost illuminates the paper (Figure 6-8).

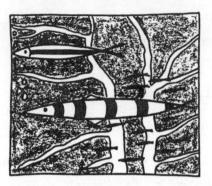

Figure 6-8

9. Pastels with Crayon

Materials: pastels; crayons; 12" X 18" white paper; newspaper; pencil.

* Cover the work area with newspaper.
* Now, with pencil, draw a pre-planned sketch on the white paper.
* With the crayon, fill in most of the picture area.
* When the picture is near completion, fill in the areas with pastel to add highlights to the picture. The delicate hue of the pastel lends an interesting contrast to the combination of crayon and pastel (Figure 6-9).

Figure 6-9

10. Pastels and Paint

Materials: tempera paint; brushes; pastels; 18" X 24" white or colored construction paper; newspaper; pencil.

* Cover the work area with newspaper.
* Now, with pencil, sketch a pre-planned idea on the 18" X 24" paper. (This technique of the pastel-paint marriage makes a most impressive still-life project.)
* When the sketch has been drawn, paint the entire picture plan.
* After the paint has dried, use the pastels, the same color as the paint, directly over portions of the painted areas.
* The contrast of the pastel in paint creates a textural pattern that gives the picture wonderful highlights (Figure 6-10).

Figure 6-10

Let's Experiment with Pastels

7

Yarn, String and
Wire Creations

The uses of yarn, string and wire have within recent years taken on an important role in classroom art. Their added use produces a fresh new approach to some of the older techniques, and their involvement in some of the newer art ideas have given them a permanent position in the art curriculum.

The fact that yarn, string and wire can easily be obtained adds to their popularity. There are always odd bits of yarn, string and wire to be found around a home. It is a wise teacher who puts out a request for these items; some really wonderful art creations can result from their use.

A. TECHNIQUES USING YARN, STRING AND WIRE

1. Stitchery on Orange Mesh Bags

Materials: mesh bags (store containers for oranges and grapefruit); assorted-colored yarn; large-eyed needles; scissors; manila paper; pencil; felt-tip marker.

* If the bag is left in its original shape, let the design be created in a free, spontaneous way by just sewing the colored yarn in and out, forming pleasing colored patterns around the bag (Figure 7-1).
* However, small picture hangings can be made if the mesh bag is cut into squares and rectangles.

* To do this, draw a simple sketch on a piece of manila paper the same size as the mesh.
* Then lay the sketch under the mesh and trace the picture on the mesh with felt-tip marker.
* When the sketch has been repeated on the mesh, thread a large-eyed needle with yarn and begin sewing in and out of the holes, defining the black lines of the marker with the colored yarn.
* Areas of the yarn picture will be made more interesting if they are filled in with the yarn (Figure 7-2).

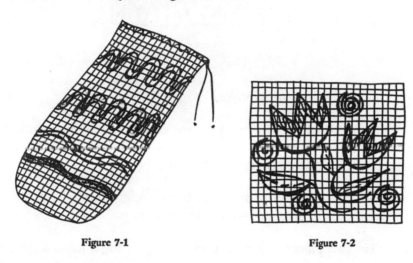

Figure 7-1   Figure 7-2

2. Stitchery on Burlap Hangings

Materials: burlap squares or rectangles about 12″ X 18″ in size; assorted-colored yarn; large-eyed needle; pencil; manila paper; felt-tip marker.

* Draw a pre-planned idea on the manila paper the same size as the burlap.
* Transfer the picture idea to the burlap with felt-tip marker. If the marker does not show up on the burlap, outline the picture in white chalk.
* Thread the needle with yarn and begin to stitch color into the burlap picture.
* Try experimenting with a variety of stitches. It is fun to see how many new stitches can be integrated into the design of the picture (Figure 7-3).

Figure 7-3

3. God's Eyes (O'jos de Dios)

O'jos de Dios, or God's Eyes, are constructions that come to us from a group of Mexican Indians. They are colorful, woven designs that make beautiful hanging ornaments.

> Materials: wood shapes, such as twigs, toothpicks, popsicle sticks, thin dowels; assorted yarn; scissors.

* Tie two pieces of wood, even in length, together in a cross or X fashion.
* Now tie the yarn in the center and begin the weaving by wrapping the yarn around one stick on the cross and then spanning the yarn to the next stick on the cross.
* Continue this procedure, changing the color scheme and yarn texture from time to time for interest.
* When the cross is complete, cut and fasten the end of the yarn to the cross with a small knot.
* Add beads or wool pom-poms at the stick ends for added decoration (Figure 7-4).

4. Painting with Yarn

> Materials: assorted-colored yarn, string or cord; wallpaper paste or white school paste diluted with water; scissors; waxed paper; newspaper; container for paste.

* Cover the work area with newspaper.

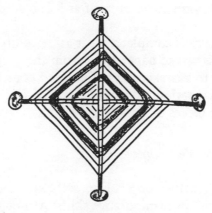

Figure 7-4

* Place a sheet of waxed paper over this. This is the background paper.
* With the tip of the scissors, sketch a simple picture of an animal, bird, flower or fish in the waxed paper.
* Now cut the yarn into 12" lengths.
* Take a piece of yarn and dip it into the paste mixture.
* Pull it out carefully and squeeze it between two fingers as you remove it from the container. This will rid the string of excess paste.
* Now lay the wet yarn in the incised lines of the sketch.
* Continue to add the yarn to the lines of the picture, filling in some areas solidly and allowing freedom of space in others.
* Outline, coil and arrange the yarn in interesting designs of color.

Figure 7-5

Yarn, String and Wire Creations

* Make sure the yarn touches itself as it is placed next to another piece of yarn.
* When the picture is complete, set it aside to dry.
* Cut the excess waxed paper away from the yarn picture when it is dry. Attach it to a background of colored construction paper.
* For added decoration, add beads, bits of lace, crumpled tissue paper, ribbon or pieces of glass (Figure 7-5).

5. Weaving on Simple Looms

Weaving offers creative originality, self-expression and excellent development in a child's manipulative skills. Although the techniques are ancient and fairly basic, they challenge the student with any number of varied possibilities that he can create and discover.

a. Cardboard Looms

One of the nicest and most inexpensive ways to adapt weaving for practical use with children is with the aid of a simply constructed cardboard *loom*.

Materials: Cardboard rectangle, any size; scissors; assorted-colored yarn; shuttle (which could be a bobby pin or a tongue depressor with a slit cut in each end to wind the yarn around); ruler; pencil; tape.

* Cut the cardboard shape. A rectangle or square of any size is fine.
* Measure and mark with a dot the top and bottom of the cardboard at ½" intervals.
* Then cut notches about ½" deep at each dot. The loom is ready for warp.
* Now knot a piece of the yarn to the end of the first notch at the top of the loom. Run the yarn down to the bottom of the cardboard, and place it under and around the first notch at the bottom. Bring the yarn up the front of the loom to the second notch at the top. Place it in and around the notch and down in front again to the second notch at the bottom of the cardboard.
* Continue to do this until the entire cardboard loom has been strung with the yarn. At the last notch, secure the end of the yarn with a knot.
* The yarn threads that are strung on the loom are the *warp* threads of the loom (Figure 7-6).

* Now fasten a piece of masking tape over the ends of the loom — top and bottom — so the warp ends will be secure and not slide off the cardboard loom.
* The loom is now ready for weaving.
* Fasten the yarn to the shuttle.
* Now begin weaving under and over the warp on the loom. The weaving of the horizontal threads becomes the weft or *woof* of the design. Expose the warp in some areas and insert bits of natural materials such as small sticks, bones or reed pieces within the warp for an exciting treatment (Figure 7-7).

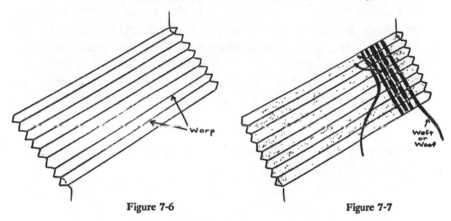

Figure 7-6   Figure 7-7

* Remember to always push the weft closely together to form a tightly woven pattern.
* When the weaving is complete, remove it from the cardboard loom by simply pulling off the tape and bending the cardboard shape carefully so the warp loops can be slipped off.

b. Weave a Belt — Plastic Drinking-Straw Loom

Materials: two plastic soda straws for each loom; scissors; yarn.

* Cut each straw in half so there are four pieces of straw.
* Now cut four pieces of yarn at least two sizes larger than the size of the weaver's waist, and string them in each straw.
* Tie a knot at the top of each of the pieces of yarn and attach a button to it so the yarn will not pull through the straw. This becomes the warp.
* Next, connect all the bottom ends of the four pieces of yarn with an overhand knot. The loom is complete.

Yarn, String and Wire Creations

* Now tie a ball of yarn to one of the outside straws. This is the weft or woof.
* Hold the four straws together in one hand and, with the other hand, begin to work the weft over and under the straw loom (Figure 7-8a).
* When the yarn reaches the last straw, wind it around to the back and work in and out, with the yarn returning to its original position.
* Continue to repeat the procedure, adding more weft whenever needed by just an addition of yarn tied to the old weft.
* Push the woven material down the straws as the weaving proceeds, but never let the woven area ride off the straw loom. Some weaving must always remain on the straw loom while the weaving is in progress.
* Change colors and thicknesses of the yarn. Form an interesting pattern in the weaving as the work is being done.
* When the belt is complete, remove the straws and make an overhand knot with the warp strands.
* Beads or more yarn fringes can be added to the belt ends for decoration (Figure 7-8b).

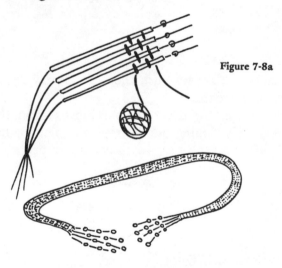

Figure 7-8a

Figure 7-8b

The width of the weaving depends entirely upon the number of straws that are used for the loom. I have had students who have woven on a 10-straw loom. This size makes a wonderful muffler.

c. Thread Spool Loom

This little loom uses an old technique that I am sure we all enjoyed as youngsters. Times have not changed. The children of today are still fascinated by the spool loom or, as it is sometimes called, the Horse Reign weaving loom.

Materials: a wooden thread spool (obtained from mother); yarn; large safety pin; small 1" nails; hammer.

* Have each child hammer four nails into the wooden spool, forming an X pattern.
* Drop a yarn-end down the middle of the spool. This is the tail or end of the weaving.
* Now wind the yarn around each nail one time before going to the next nail.
* When all four have been wound, the yarn is back to the first nail.
* Lay the yarn above the bottom loop and slip the bottom loop over the top yarn and nail head with the safety pin. This makes one stitch.
* Move to the next nail and repeat the process (Figure 7-9a).
* Periodically, pull down the tail. This keeps the loom center taut.

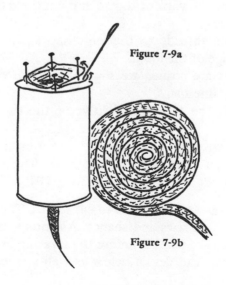

Figure 7-9a

Figure 7-9b

* Continue to slip the bottom loop over the new yarn and off the nail until the knitting, which is being formed, comes out at the bottom of the spool.
* The knitted rope can be circled and sewn to be used as mats, belts, pot holders or nice long jumping ropes (Figure 7-9b).

6. String Designs on Simple Permanent Looms

Materials: large sheet of stiff cardboard; scissors; assorted colors and thicknesses of yarn, thread, or cord; pieces of cardboard tube; pieces of cardboard; ruler; pencil; duco cement.

* Cut the cardboard sheet into an interesting shape. This will be the permanent loom.
* Place measurement dots at ½" intervals all around the loom.
* Cut slits of ½" at every dot.
* Now glue a piece of cardboard tube onto one area of the loom, the open side up.
* Make another larger circular or geometric shape from a strip of cardboard and glue this to another area on the loom.
* Carefully cut slits in the top of the round shapes at ½" intervals.
* Knot a piece of cord to one of the slits and run it from one side of the cardboard loom to the other.
* Cut other cords, yarn or thread and continue to run the lines in other directions.
* Fasten some threads to the large and small circles, and then back to the edge of the loom.
* As the lines are strung, tie simple knots in the woof to form textures in the line spans.
* Do not pull the cord too tightly, or the cardboard loom will buckle.
* Weave the string pattern into the loom until you are satisfied with the design that has been formed. The result will be an attractive abstract composition (Figure 7-10).

String designs are not confined to cut looms. They can be made on boxes and lids of all sizes and shapes. An interesting addition to the permanent loom is to paint it before the weaving begins; then there is a movement from the design below as well as the string movement above it.

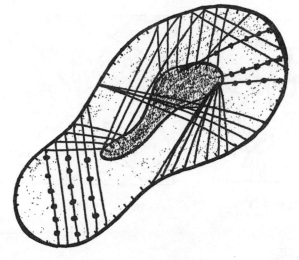

Figure 7-10

7. String Painting

Materials: string, cut about 12″ long; container of tempera paint; manila paper; newspaper; ruler.

* Cover the work area with newspaper.
* Fold the manila paper in half; then reopen it.
* Dip the string into the container of paint.
* Slowly pull it out squeezing the string between the container and a ruler to remove the excess paint.
* Lay the string on one side of the folded paper; allow a little tail of the string to hang out at the bottom. This will be the string that you pull later. Now cover it with the other half of the paper.
* Rub your hand over the top of the folded paper and start to wiggle and pull the tail of the string slowly away from the folded paper.
* Open the folded paper. The string has left an interesting symmetrical design on each half of the folded paper (Figure 7-11)

Another variation of string painting is to dip the string in paint and drag it while it is loaded with paint over the surface of the paper. Repeat the process by using different colors on the string that is used (Figure 7-12).

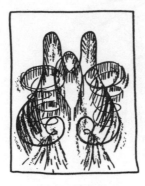

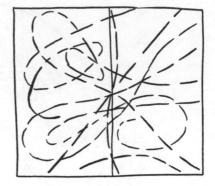

Figure 7-11   Figure 7-12

8. Wire Stabiles

Materials: wire that is easy to bend and manipulate, such as aluminum, steel, or plastic-coated electric wire; wire cutters or old scissors; tape; block of wood; pliers; glue.

* Cut the wire into 3-foot lengths. Tape the ends for protective purposes.
* Make a hole in the wood block with the point blade of the scissors.
* Put one end of the wire in the hole and fasten it with a drop of glue.
* Now use any point on the wire for the start of the *stabile*. Experiment with the wire to decide where you want to actually start the creation.
* When working with wire, it is best to carry out the form in as free a manner as possible. However, if a certain shape is desired, a form can be used as a base around which to wrap the wire; then, when the form is removed, the wire will hold that specific shape. For example, a box or wood block can be used for a square shape; wire can be wrapped around a pencil to form a small coil; a tube can be used to make a circular shape. Experimenting with shapes around which to wrap the wire can be an interesting experience, too.
* Check all aspects of the stabile as the wire is formed. Change the movement of the wire from time to time. Curve, bend, pinch and twist the wire. Make it static or movable with the aid of the pliers or with your hands.

* Allow spaces in the shape. Add other pieces of wire by twisting the new piece to the shape, or by pinching the two pieces together with pliers.

* Continue to work on the shape until it is exciting to look at from all angles (Figure 7-13).

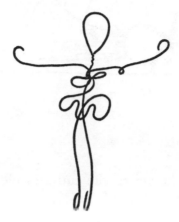

Figure 7-13

* The wire stabile, when completed, can remain in its natural form or new dimensions can be created by pouring a thin solution of plaster of Paris over the shape or drippings from a lighted candle can be dropped on areas of the wire shape for another interesting possibility.

9. Wire Pictures

Materials: soft wire; scissors; tape; duco cement; hammer; block of wood; 12" by 18" lightweight cardboard; crayons.

* Cut the wire into pieces of about 18" in length.

* Play with the wire and try to develop an interesting shape, such as a person, animal, bird or building.

* Bend, coil and twist the wire to form the shape desired.

* If the wire shape is not pleasing, it can be hammered smooth on a block of wood.

* When a shape is complete, glue or tape it to the cardboard.

* Add several shapes if the picture warrants it.

* Now *unify* the picture of wire shapes with a suitable crayon background (Figure 7-14).

Yarn, String and Wire Creations

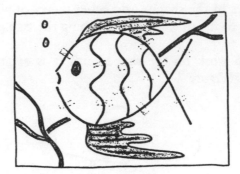

Figure 7-14

10. Wire Jewelry

Materials: wire; hammer; wire cutter or old pair of scissors; pin or earring findings; block of wood; pencil; tweezers.

* Cut the wire into lengths of 18″.
* Carefully wrap the wire around a pencil to form a tight coil.
* Take the pencil base away from the wire coil and gently make an appealing shape. Use the tweezers to spread the coil whenever necessary.
* If the coil is not satisfactory, hammer it smooth on the block of wood and reshape the wire.
* Attach the wire shapes to the pin or earring findings with just a twist of the wire around the base of the finding.
* Add pieces of stone, mirror or aluminum foil for added interest.

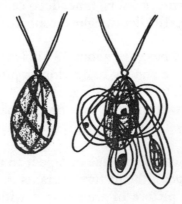

Figure 7-15

* When making a wire ring, form three or more coils around a pencil. Then flatten them on the wood block and twist or braid the rest of the wire together until the ring size is obtained.
* Now bend the twist or braid around to the coils and attach with a twist to form the ring or circle shape.
* Combine colored wire together for an interesting pattern of color.
* Small stones, chips of glass or tiny pieces of mirror can be glued to the center of the coils for added decoration (Figure 7-15).

11. Wiggly Shaped Constructions

Materials: soft wire; pencils; rulers; erasers; scissors; plaster of Paris; aluminum pie and cake tins; discarded large milk containers; water.

* Cut wire into several pieces about 12" long
* Now slowly wrap a piece of wire around a base, such as a pencil, ruler or eraser. Wrap it carefully and tightly so that it forms a tight coil.
* Slowly remove the coil from the base shape, and set it aside.
* Continue to make the wiggly coils until there is a variety of shapes and sizes that will make an interesting assortment.
* Now mix the plaster of Paris by slowly pouring about 1 cup of the dry plaster into about 2/3 cups of water, stirring the mixture with your hand or an old ruler until it is mixed well.
* Next, carefully pour the liquid plaster of Paris into the pie or cake molds.

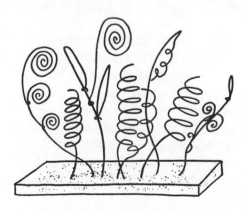

Figure 7-16

* Let the plaster set until it is just ready to completely harden. Then quickly place the end of the wigglies in a nice arrangement directly into the plaster.
* Now set the arrangement aside to dry thoroughly.
* When it is dried completely, remove the aluminum mold.
* Paint the plaster with tempera for a more colorful composition if desired (Figure 7-16).

12. Macrame Belt

Materials: any cord, rug yarn or twine; scissors; a piece of beaver board about 14" X 18" in size, or a rectangle of *Styrofoam*; large pins such as T pins or glass ball-headed pins; glue; crochet hook; elastic bands.

Macrame is an enchanting old craft that has recently regained much popularity. It originated as an ancient sailor's pastime, but is now enjoyed by female and child as well. With the knowledge of just a few basic knots, there are innumerable designs and projects that anyone can make.

Here is a delightful belt that can be made simply by using a single knot in a repeated pattern. Children will love doing it.

* Cut four cords about 30" longer than the person's waist measurement. (For instance, if a waist measurement is 22" the cords should each be 52" long.)
* Now cut two cords about five times the length of the other cords. (In this case it would be about 260".)
* Roll the two cords into little balls and fasten all the balls with elastic bands.
* Now make an overhand knot with all six cords (Figure 7-17a.) and pin the knot to the work surface. (The work surface is the beaver board or the Styrofoam rectangle.)
* Next place the cords so the two long cords are on either side of the four shorter cords.
* Now proceed to tie the two long cords around the four middle cords in a half knot. (Figure 7-17b.)
* The half knot when continuously tied begins to form a delightful twist. Help the twist by just turning the knot when a twist forms.
* When more cord is needed for the knotting release it from the elastic band.

* Continue to knot until the waist measurement is reached.
* At this point make another overhand knot with the six strands and the belt is completed. (Figure 7-17c.)
* Add beads, shells or buttons for added decorations on the end strands of the belt.
* When the children become proficient with the Half Knot, let them experiment with the Square Knot and the Half Hitch. (Figure 7-17d and 17e.)
* Combinations of the knots will make other more intricate belt patterns.

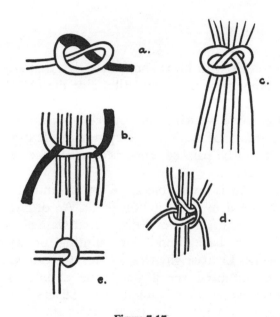

Figure 7-17

8

Stones, Wood and Reed...
Let's Work with Nature!

This chapter deals with ideas about materials that are easy to find and whose manipulation and completion give the child-artist a great deal of satisfaction.

The common stone, which is an object of beauty in itself, can be utilized in a number of ways for art purposes. It can be used in a construction; it can be painted, crayoned, used in jewelry or used as tesserae in a mosiac.

Wood in all forms is invaluable as an art medium. Scrap pieces of all sorts can be used in construction work. An ordinary, discarded flat plank or a piece of driftwood discovered washed up on a beach can be used as a background for painting or as a base for construction work. Lightweight wood — balsa — can be purchased at a nominal fee and used for a stabile or mobile. The common household toothpick becomes a unique material as a building tool.

Reed, which is primarily used for weaving, can be utilized in the classroom as a material for making a mobile, construction or kite.

Figure 8-1

This chapter will attempt to give the reader some new and some forgotten suggestions about the use of nature's stones, wood and reed. They are materials that children like to work with and collect. Give the children you are working with an opportunity to explore fully with nature's offerings to the art world.

A. HOW TO WORK WITH STONES, WOOD AND REED

1. Paint on Stones

Creating an art work with a mere stone is one of the most exciting and rewarding lessons that can be done in a classroom. From the time of the lesson's inception, the children become involved in the search for the basic materials needed: stones. This involvement makes the interest increase steadily even before the designated project is in progress.

Materials: collection of assorted shapes and colors of stones; acrylic paints; brushes; water; container.

* Wash the stones of particles of soil and moss before the lesson.
* Have the children choose a stone from the collection that is pleasing to the eye and touch.
* Suggest that the stone be examined carefully and looked at from all angles to find a position of the stone that fits an idea conceived by the students. Perhaps when examining the stone it will be discovered to have an unusual shape that suggests an idea.
* Finding portions of a stone that represents familiar objects will become a challenge to the child. Before long he will discover shapes that offer all sorts of possibilities when they are aided slightly. For example, the entire shape of a stone might suggest the body of a cat or squirrel. A portion of the stone might jut out and be considered a nose, ear or chin.
* Aid the proposed idea whenever possible with a splash of color for a mouth, arm or leg; all sorts of unexpected happenings occur.
* Soon the stone takes on the appearance of a recognizable animal, bird or fish shape (Figure 8-1).
* If acrylics are not available, use tempera paints or felt-tip markers instead; and after allowing the paint to dry thoroughly, coat the stone with polymer medium or shellac for a protective shiny surface.

2. Crayon on Stones

Materials: a collection of flat-surfaced stones in a variety of colors, shapes and sizes; crayons; scrap paper; polymer medium or shellac; brushes; pencil.

* Wash the stones of particles of soil and moss before the lesson.
* Choose a plain, flat-surfaced stone that will make a wonderful background for a simple design.
* First, on scrap paper, draw a simple sketch of an idea that might be interesting on the stone.
* Now lightly repeat the sketch on the stone with the pencil.
* Then start to fill in areas of the planned design with heavy crayon, always considering the color of the stone with the color scheme of the design.
* When the stone is adequately crayoned, give it a coat of shellac or polymer to preserve the picture (Figure 8-2).

Figure 8-2

3. Stone Constructions

Materials: a collection of stones in a variety of different colors, sizes and shapes; duco cement; acrylic paint; brushes; scraps of felt; felt-tip markers; scissors; miscellaneous "goodies" such as bits of lace, ribbons, beads or feathers.

* First, wash all the stones of particles of soil and moss.
* Each child should have an assortment of stones with which to work. There should also be an exchange table with excess stones

on it available to those who do not have a good supply of suitable stones in their collection.

* Suggest that the children experiment with building the stones into shapes of some sort, such as stone creatures, animals or birds. Two stones, one a body and another a head, make a wonderful start. The children will soon learn that it is important to balance one stone upon another in the process of constructing. For instance, it would be almost impossible to fasten a huge stone on top of a much smaller one if they did not balance, even when glued.

* After experimenting for a period of time, the children will be eager to fasten their stones together permanently by applying duco cement to the crucial balancing points.

* When the glue on the larger stone has been given a chance to dry, smaller stones can then be added with more glue for the arms and legs of these little creatures.

* Again, let the glue dry thoroughly and then add paint in needed areas for accentuation and decoration.

* In addition to the paint, pieces of cut felt, buttons, lace and other "goodies" can be glued on to enhance the construction (Figure 8-3).

Figure 8-3

4. Pebble or Stone Mosaic

Mosiac is one of the oldest decorative media. It is an art technique that is to be respected and done with much care and planning. The technique involves skill, and one should work with tesserae, mortar and grout on a sturdy background, using either the direct or indirect method.

A simplified "mock" mosaic method, which I will describe for use in the classroom, is a technique that employs glue to set the tesserae on a designated background. Although the finished piece is just a playful decoration, it does help give the children the mosaic concept.

The tesserae are the small pieces that are used to make the design or picture in mosaic, and all kinds of materials can be used as the tesserae in a classroom. Some common materials that are used are pebbles, stones, shells, seeds, paste, bits of colored paper and tissue.

Materials: pebbles or small stones; glue; sturdy cardboard, about 12″ X 18″, cut from large cartons or a similarly sized piece of plywood; scrap paper; pencil.

* Prior to the lesson, collect a good supply of pebbles from a beach area or go to a lumber supply house and purchase a bag of pebbles at a nominal fee. (Having a commercial bag of pebbles on hand is an excellent idea, especially for those children who are unable to supply a sufficient number of stones for themselves.) The pebbles are the tesserae for the lesson's mosaic.
* Each child will need a piece of extra-sturdy cardboard or a piece of plywood for the background.
* On a piece of scrap paper the same size as the background, plan a design for the mosaic project. Any subject can be used. Possibilities might include: fish; birds; family pets; large, simple flowers; or just a good design.
* When the sketch is satisfactory, transfer the idea directly to the background form with a pencil.
* Next, place the pebbles in a suitable area near the background for planned attachment.
* When setting the tesserae (pebbles) on the sketched area, first place a small portion of glue in an area of the picture. Then take a handful of the pebbles and begin to set them on the background in the glue as they come to hand, but attempt to set them with the nicest side of the pebble up. Work slowly and in small areas — a little at a time.
* Continue the procedure by first placing glue and then tesserae into the outlined areas of the picture.
* Keep the stones in rhythm of direction and in basic color themes as the mosaic progresses. Work to the edges of the design with the tesserae.
* If, during the progress of the work, a flaw is noticed either in

color or tesserae position, pry the stone in that area out of the design and proceed to alter the area.

* The completed mosaic can be framed for hanging or left as it is. In its original state in can be propped on its side on a shelf for vertical viewing (Figure 8-4).

Figure 8-4

5. Etching on Slate

Slate is a "sleeper" in that it is not often enough considered for use in an art lesson. However, if you give it a chance, it becomes a wonderful art medium with which to work. Contrary to belief, this material is easily obtainable at little or no cost.

When we planned to work with slate in our classroom, we visited garden shops in the immediate area of the school. We found at once that we were able to obtain as much slate as we wanted without any fee at all, just by asking for scrap pieces. We also discovered that parents would contribute pieces of slate from their excess garden supplies.

Materials: slate (blue and black slate is best for *etching*); an old screw driver, nails or scissors; chalk; fine-grade sandpaper; hard wax; soft rag; scrap paper; pencil.

* First, sketch a picture on the scrap paper.
* When the sketch is pleasing, transfer it to the slate with chalk lines. (An undesirable sketch can easily be rubbed off the slate.)
* Now outline the chalk lines with a sharp-pointed tool. Continue

to use pressure around the outline until the shape is adequately defined.

* Next, chip the slate away carefully around the outlined area until the drawn shape is in relief.

* How much slate is taken away depends entirely upon the student-artist.

* Chipping the slate away may appear difficult, but it is not. The slate is soft and layered, so this is an easy task. However, the project is one that must be done slowly and carefully if it is to be done correctly.

* A pattern can be developed in the background area by manipulating the sharp tool in various ways.

* When the relief-picture appears complete, carefully sand the slate picture (not the background) with fine-grade sandpaper until it is smooth.

* Next, apply a thin coat of hard wax to the picture and buff it with a soft rag until the surface becomes shiny.

* Complete the project by either carefully piercing a hole through the top of the slate picture so it can be hung, or by mounting it with glue to a sturdy board (Figure 8-5).

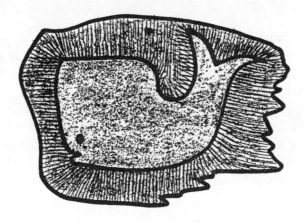

Figure 8-5

6. Paint on Wood

A flat piece of board found at the beach or in the scrap barrels of a lumber yard makes a wonderful surface for a painted picture or design. If the wood has an interesting shape or size, all the better!

Materials: flat board that is any size or shape; watercolor paints; brushes; pencil; scrap paper; water; container.

* First, draw a sketch on the scrap paper of the proposed idea for the board.
* When the sketch is pleasing, transfer it to the board lightly with pencil.
* After the design areas are indicated, begin to paint the areas with the tempera.
* Use the paint with as little water as possible. Too much water may create unnecessary *bleeding* (Figure 8-6).
* When the painting is complete, fasten eye screws to the back of the board for hanging purposes.

Figure 8-6

7. Scrap-Wood Construction

Children, no matter what age, love working with pieces of wood. If at all possible, there should be a work bench with a vise in each classroom. If this is not possible, the work bench should be somewhere in an empty room or the nook of a hallway, so that children can go to the table and just pound nails into pieces of wood.

It is understandable that having a work bench and its advantages is not always possible (especially if some form of supervision and help is not available), but the next best solution would be to be able to build a construction in the classroom. If nails and hammers are an impossibility, glue can be used as a substitute adhering medium.

Wood is costly, but local lumber yards are usually most co-operative in donating their wood scraps for just the asking. Another valuable source of lumber would be the scraps that are salvaged from new housing developments.

Materials: lumber scraps; glue; saw; nails; hammer; paint; easel brushes; masking tape.

* Have a discussion prior to the wood-building about the possibilities than can be utilized when making a construction. Stress the fact that a wood construction can be almost anything — an animal, bird, house, table, car, train, etc.
* Lay the wood scraps out in a large, open area.
* When the child feels he has a designated idea in his mind relative to the construction, allow him to choose the wood scraps he feels necessary for his work from the assortment on hand.
* Now let him assemble his wood in either one of three ways: by connecting the pieces with hammer and nails; by gluing; or by a combination of the two techniques. If glue is used it may be advantageous to tape the pieces with masking tape after they are glued to give them extra support until the glue is dry. Then the tape can be removed.
* When the construction is complete, it can be painted. Use tempera paint for younger children, followed by shellac for preservation. Older children can use enamel paint and omit the shellac.
* Yarn or felt scraps can be added to the construction with glue for extra decoration (Figure 8-7).

Figure 8-7

8. Wood-and-Nail Design

Materials: a piece of ¾" or 1" plywood, no smaller than 12" X 18" in size; hammer; an assortment of nails, about ¾" to 3" in size, that are made of various metals and with different head shapes; newspaper; manila paper the size of the board; pencil; paint; brushes; shellac.

* Draw a design on the manila paper that will cover the entire area.
* Carefully transfer the design idea to the plywood with the pencil.
* Cover the working area with a thick pad of newspaper to absorb the sound of the nail pounding, and also to prevent over-ambitious hammerers from pounding nails in too far.
* Now begin to outline areas of the design with various nails.
* When the outlines have been made with the nails, begin to enclose areas with different types and sizes of nails (small nails to be placed in the design first).
* Experimentation will soon teach the child that the nails cannot be placed too closely together (the wood areas will drop out). Also, the nails cannot be pounded in too far, nor can they be pounded in too lightly (they will pop off).
* The work is noisy, tedious and a bit monotonous. However, when the nail design is complete, it is a most attractive endeavor (Figure 8-8).

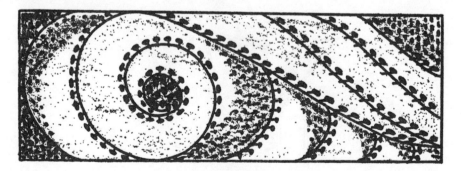

Figure 8-8

* The final project can remain in its natural form or it can be painted or shellacked.

* A *frame* can be placed around the board or two eye-screws can be fastened to the sides for hanging.

9. Balsa-Wood Construction

Materials: balsa-wood strips in various widths; glue; small kitchen knife; straight pins; colored cellophane or tissues; scissors; paint; brushes.

* Cut the balsa strips into a variety of lengths.
* A good beginning base is made by fastening two pieces of balsa wood together in the shape of an L with a bit of glue, and fortifying it with a straight pin. (When applying the glue, note that a thin coat of glue will dry sooner and therefore be more effective than using a larger quantity of glue.)
* Now set this aside to dry and begin to construct other shapes such as squares, triangles and rectangles. As each is made set it aside to dry.
* When joining pieces that do not form an L, cut the ends on a slant and they will fasten together more easily.
* When there is a collection of various shapes that are dry and secure, take out the pins and begin to fasten the shapes together.
* Be sure that the supports are effectively planned as a part of the entire design.

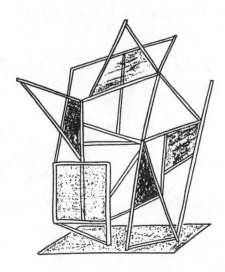

Figure 8-9

* Build interesting planes out and up. When the construction has reached a satisfactory size, emphasize the volume with pieces of cut tissue or cellophane glued to the wood.
* Portions of the construction can be painted with tempera as a contrast to the natural balsa texture (Figure 8-9).

10. Tongue-Depressor Bracelet

Materials: tongue depressor; glass; pan; water; paint; brushes; shellac; beads; buttons; glue.

* Fill a pan half full with water.
* Soak the tongue depressors in the water for several hours, or overnight.
* After soaking the tongue depressor, which is merely a sliver of wood, it will be most flexible.
* Bend the depressor around to form a circle and slip it into a glass with a straight side to dry (Figure 8-10a).
* When the wood dries it will take the shape of the glass into which it was placed: round and in the form of a bracelet. It will be quite sturdy, and it will be flexible enough to open and slide on the wrist.
* Decorate the bracelet with tempera paint.
* It is most attractive if it is first painted a solid color. Then, when it is dry, additional designs in other colors can be applied in desired areas.
* The placement of an occasional bead or small, fancy stone glued to a painted area makes the bracelet quite exciting (Figure 8-10b).

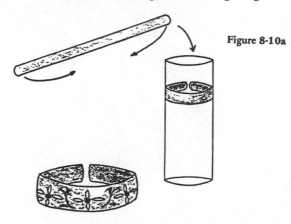

Figure 8-10a

Figure 8-10b

* A coat of shellac covering the entire bracelet will make it a more permanent project.

11. Tongue-Depressor Book Mark

Materials: tongue depressors; paint; brushes; crayon; shellac; scrap paper; pencil.

* Outline the tongue depressor on the scrap paper several times.
* Now experiment with each outlined shape.
* Draw designs on some, print words on others, or put little pictures on others.
* When the ideas are pleasing, transfer them directly to the wood with light pencil.
* Then decide whether paint or crayon is more suitable for your idea, and proceed to work in the medium chosen.
* If crayon is used, the appearance can be changed entirely by placing a piece of paper over the crayoned area and pressing it with a warm iron. The wax and color in the crayon melt into the wood and create vibrant color.
* Areas of this design can be outlined with felt-tip marker to create a stained-glass window look. The marker will not run because the melted crayon will act as a sealer on the surface of the wood (Figure 8-11).

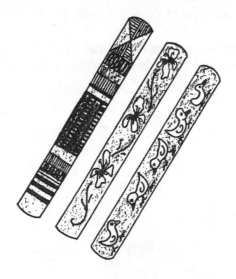

Figure 8-11

12. Toothpick Construction

Materials: toothpicks; glue; a base (which could be a rectangle or square of sturdy cardboard, a piece of plastic foam or a wad of plasticene or clay); paint; brushes.

* If foam or clay is being used as a base, anchor some toothpicks directly onto the material. These form the foundation of the construction.
* If cardboard is used, place a small amount of glue on each of three toothpicks — top and bottom — and use them as a beginning foundation set together in tent fashion.
* Now slowly and carefully add to the base toothpicks. A light coat of glue applied to each toothpick will dry more quickly and make a sturdier construction.
* Continue to add toothpicks, continuously building out and up, forming many interesting angles and planes.
* When the construction has reached a satisfactory size, it can be painted or left in its natural state (Figure 8-12).

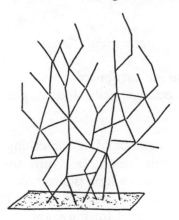

Figure 8-12

13. Toothpick-and-Reed Construction

Materials: toothpicks; glue; basket reed; scissors; 5″ X 10″ corrugated board.

* Cut the reed into lengths of about 16″ X 18″.
* Carefully bend the reed and insert the ends into the side slots of

the corrugated board. Reinforce the entry with a drop of glue.

* Now carefully place glue at intervals on the curved forms of the reed and place the toothpicks on the glued area. Spiral, tilt and cluster the pieces of wood to form interesting shapes.

* Continue to add glue and toothpicks until a pleasing growth and shape is made (Figure 8-13).

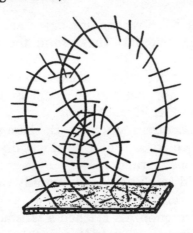

Figure 8-13

14. Toothpick Construction with Candy

Materials: wood or cardboard base; compass; tempera paint; brushes; duco cement; jelly beans; gum drops; tiny marshmallows.

* A construction means building something, and that is precisely what is done in this lesson. It is not the usual construction; however, in it we are combining the common household toothpick and candy of some sort in order to build. The candy in this case becomes the adhering agent for the shape.

* Give each child a compass, a pile of toothpicks and the candy of their choice, and the creation can start.

* Make the base by putting a piece of candy on each end of a toothpick. (If the toothpick does not readily go into the candy, pierce it first with a compass point.)

* Add to the construction by continuing to build onto it with more candy and toothpicks until a definite pattern is formed. Build the shape out and up with many open spaces. Avoid tightly closed areas (Figure 8-14).

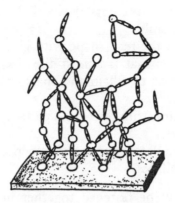

Figure 8-14

* The construction can be as large or small as the builder wishes it to be.

* When it is complete, it can be attached to a wood or cardboard bottom with a bit of glue for more durability.

* If added color is desired, paint the toothpicks and base with tempera paint.

15. Reed Mobiles

A *mobile* is a three-dimensional design that will move in space. It can be made of a variety of materials, but here is a good, lightweight and inexpensive mobile that does not need tedious balancing and can be made readily in a classroom.

Materials: basket reed #2, cut in lengths of 24"; scissors; scotch tape or lightweight wire; colored cellophane or tissue; rubber cement; string.

* Suggest that the children experiment with bending and shaping a piece of reed. The reed is quite pliable and does not have to be soaked in water before use. Since it is taken from a coil, it will naturally take on a circular shape. However, it can be twisted and turned into an oval or leaf shape.

* After a desirable reed shape is made, tape or wire the ends together so that the shape remains secure.

* Continue to make other reed shapes until there is a good basis for the mobile. Other shapes can be made later if necessary.

* Now start to consider colors that will be harmonious in the total design of the mobile.
* Cover one side of the reed shape with glue and cover the area with a piece of paper that is almost the size of the reed. Set it aside to dry and start to fill in the spaces made by other reed shapes with more paper.
* When the glue is dry, trim the excess paper away from the shape with a pair of scissors.
* Now take the completed shapes and experiment with them. Try some of these possibilities:

1. The shapes may be fastened together in a chain formation (Figure 8-15a).
2. The shapes can be fastened into groups to form butterflies, fish or flowers, and hung from a string (Figure 8-15b).
3. The shapes can be attached with tape to straight pieces of reed and balanced to make an interesting, large mobile (Figure 8-15c).
4. The shapes can be attached to straight pieces of reed and placed in a wad of clay for a stationary project. This is called a stabile (Figure 8-15d).

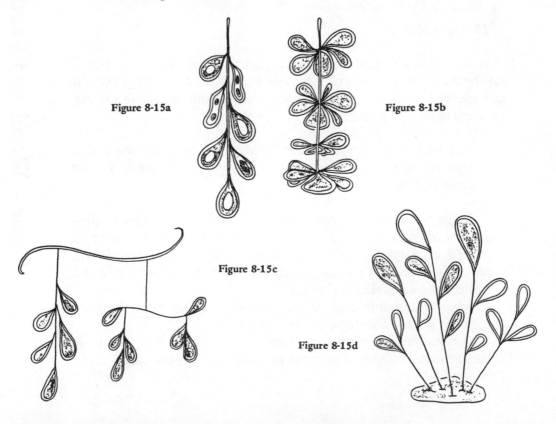

Figure 8-15a

Figure 8-15b

Figure 8-15c

Figure 8-15d

16. Reed Kites

Everyone loves to fly a kite. All types can be purchased, but a kite that is actually made by a child is one that will always be cherished as the very best.

Materials: heavyweight reed, one piece about 34″ X 36″, the other about 28″ to 30″; pencil; mural paper; string; tempera paint; brushes; crayons; scissors; rubber cement.

* Put a pencil mark in the middle of the short piece of reed, and another pencil mark about 7″ or 8″ from the top of the longer piece of reed.
* Now fasten the two pieces of reed together at these pencil marks with the string tied securely. A dab of glue at this fastening will make the kite more durable.
* Now lay the cross of reed on the floor and fasten string from one point of the reed-cross to another to form a closed shape. Make sure the string is taut (Figure 8-16a).

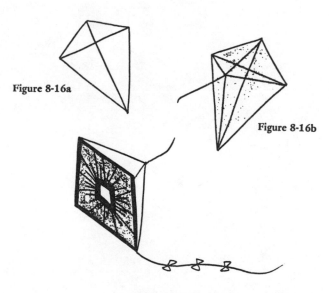

Figure 8-16a

Figure 8-16b

Figure 8-16c

* Lay the shape on mural paper and trace it with a border around it approximately 2″ wider than the actual shape.

* Now cut out the shape and decorate it with tempera paint or crayon designs.

* After the decorating has been done and the paint is dry, center the reed shape in the middle of the decorated mural paper. Make sure that the back of the paper is the area with which you are working.

* Now carefully fold the paper border over the string and carefully rubber cement it all the way around the kite.

* Next, bridle the kite vertically and horizontally to the main framework of the kite with string that sticks out about 6″ from the frame (Figure 8-16b).

* Add a tail with bits of fabric. The tail and bridle of the kite may need adjusting when the kite is actually flown (Figure 8-16c).

9

New Ways with Textiles

Fabric in all forms can play an important role in the art program. Because of its versatility, there should be a box somewhere in the classroom where bits and pieces of all types of fabric can be easily obtained. Sources of this cache can be a mother who sews, a search of the neighborhood for willing donators, or just purchasing bits of fabric during a sale.

An old sheet or pillowcase is wonderful material for crayoning, painting, tie and dye, fold and dip, or batik. Pieces of treasured fabric such as satin, velvet or chiffon are magnificent as backgrounds for paint and crayon. The color becomes vivid and alive when applied to their surfaces. Burlap can be painted on, drawn on, sewn or even colored with felt-tip marker.

The small pieces of fabric often called scraps can be utilized in collage work or as props for a variety of different projects. Just the addition of a small piece of fabric will enhance the student-artists' work. In fact, when children go searching in a scrap box they are very discerning, and to find a piece of fake fur or simulated leather creates quite a stir.

A. TECHNIQUES IN THE USE OF FABRIC

The ideas in this chapter are many and varied. However, the common denominator — fabric of some sort — always remains constant. Many of the suggestions may appear difficult to attempt in the classroom; but with all the materials available and a bit of organization, their accomplishment will be most rewarding to the adult and child.

1. Paint on Fabric

Applying crayon to a piece of *textile* is fun to do; it is also quite a common procedure. However, painting on fabric with watercolor paint is a technique that is easy and lots of fun to do, although it is not attempted too frequently.

> Materials: pieces of discarded sheeting, approximately 9" X 20"; watercolor paints; pointed brush; cup of water; scrap pieces of soap; trial paper; pencil; newspaper; felt-tip marker.

* On the trial paper, draw a sketch of some simple design such as flowers, fish or birds.
* The fabric pieces are cut long and narrow (for an interesting change), so keep this in mind when arranging the design.
* Complete the sketch and then carefully transfer the idea to the fabric with a light pencil.
* Now carefully cover the work area with newspaper and begin to paint the sheeting with the watercolors.
* Before each application of paint, rub the wet brush over a piece of scrap soap. This will cut down the bleeding or fanning of the paint on the fabric.
* Use bright, showy colors in the painting.

Figure 9-1

* When the painting is complete, either outline the design with black paint and a pointed, fine brush or cover the picture with a sheet of white tissue paper and outline the picture with black felt-tip marker right through the tissue. The tissue will absorb the extra ink and prevent the marker from bleeding.

* Complete the project by attaching a dowel at the top and bottom of the fabric to create an exciting wall hanging (Figure 9-1).

2. Crayon on Fabric

Materials: discarded white sheeting cut into pieces approximately 12″ X 18″ in size; crayons; an electric iron; pad of newspapers.

* After a short discussion about crayon on fabric, suggest that the children draw designs on the fabric with heavy crayon.

* The designs drawn can cover the fabric depicting a complete scene; it can be designs or pictures in the middle of the fabric with a design in the corners; or it can also be an all-over repeated design.

* Apply the crayon heavily with the strokes going in one direction for easier application. It may help considerably to open the free hand and hold the fabric taut in the working area while the crayoning is being done with the other hand.

* Do not design too closely to the edge of the fabric.

* When the crayoning is complete, the next step is to make permanent the color in the cloth. This is done by placing the cloth, crayon side down, on a pad of newspaper.

* Then iron the back of the designed cloth until the heat of the iron melts the crayon color into the fabric (Figure 9-2).

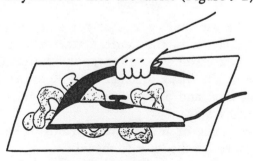

Figure 9-2

New Ways with Textiles

* The cloth can now be washed by hand without hindering the design.
* To complete the work, make a fringe at least ¾" all around the fabric. This will add a nice finishing touch to the project. (A straight pin can be of invaluable help in fringing when a stubborn thread refuses to budge in the fringing process.)

3. Tie and Dye

Children love to work in any medium involving dyes. This might even take priority over other art projects in the minds of upper elementary-grade children, and it is understandable why it is liked. The project is always enjoyable to do, and the completed item is always so impressive. Try this simple form of tie and dye and, perhaps after a try, more ambitious projects can be attempted using dyes.

> Materials: liquid dyes in a variety of different colors; large cans or enamel containers; rubber gloves; elastic bands or balls of butcher string; newspapers; scissors; pieces of fabric such as discarded sheets and pillowcases; small pebbles or coins.

* First, cut the cloth into pieces at least 18" X 24" in size.
* Each child should have cloth, string or rubber bands and scissors at his disposal.
* The adult should demonstrate various possibilities that exist when tying the fabric for tie and dye. (A few samples of finished work are also invaluable as an aid for exhibiting how a particular knot may look when completed.)
* Simple knots such as pleated knots and bull's-eye knots are probably the most advisable to introduce tie and dye in the classroom.
* When doing the bull's-eye knot you start by placing a coin or pebble in the center of the fabric. Gather the material around the shape and then carefully start to apply the elastic bands or the string close to the shape in small wind-up knots. Move down the gathered material and apply other rubber bands or tied string at intervals (Figure 9-3a).
* Use much string or many rubber bands to keep the dye from penetrating through the knot to the fabric.
* Continue to do this until you have a long cloth shape, knotted

at intervals all the way down to the bottom of the cloth (Figure 9-3b).

* For "pleat" tie-and-dye designs, fold the cloth back and forth in an accordion pleat about an inch wide, and either tie these strips in sections or fold the complete strip in half and tie this into sections (Figure 9-3c).

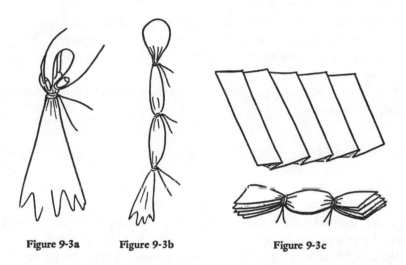

Figure 9-3a   Figure 9-3b   Figure 9-3c

* When doing random-knot tying, use both methods and tie the knots into little bundles, which will produce yet another tie-and-dye pattern.
* When the tying is complete, prepare the material for the dye bath by soaking it first in clear water for about 10 or 15 minutes.
* Then ring the excess water from the fabric and set the fabric aside.
* Now cover the work area with newspaper and don a pair of rubber gloves.
* Dissolve about half a bottle of liquid dye in a container filled with enough water to cover the proposed object being dyed.
* Make at least four different color baths.
* Now carefully dip only the tied and knotted areas into the dye bath. Use discrimination about color combinations when dipping the fabric.
* Each knotted bundle can be dipped into a different color bath, or one color can be used for all the knots.
* The excess unknotted fabric can be dipped into another color bath, but caution must be taken so the fabric area being colored

isn't dipped into the color bath too deeply, or unnecessary bleeding will occur. Sometimes this bleeding can be a blending of interesting color combinations, but it can also prove fatal to the design, so caution should be taken that the area won't be *neutralized.*

* When the dying is complete, the fabric can be taken to another newspaper-covered working area.
* Here the knots can be cut to expose the areas not dyed.
* After all the string and rubber bands are removed, hang the fabric tie and dyes to dry on a line that has previously been strung across the room.
* To complete the project, iron each piece of fabric to smooth out the wrinkles.

4. Fold and Dip

Children are always enthusiastic when they know they will be doing this lesson. It is a technique in which paper is dyed in areas that are dipped into a color bath. The folding is a very important part of good paper dying, as in the case of tie and dye work.

Fold and dip is excellent in classrooms where there are large numbers of children involved. The color vats are muffin tins and these can be shared in groups of five and six, so distribution is made simple.

Materials: tempera paint in a variety of different colors; muffin tins; pieces of paper toweling; tissue paper or rice paper; water; newspaper; rubber bands (optional).

* Cover the work area with newspaper.
* Fill the muffin tins with a mixture of water and tempera color. If more color is used, the dye will be dark. If less color is used, it will be light in color.
* Have at least six different colors in each muffin tin.
* Now experiment with folding the paper. It can be folded in many ways, but here are a few suggestions that my students have found most successful.
* Pleat the paper back and forth into a fan-fold; then bend the entire pleat in half and dip the corners, ends and sides into the color. Then carefully open the shape and lay it on the newspaper to dry (Figure 9-4a).

* Another paper fold would be to fold a square of paper in half two times. Then fold one corner to the other corner to form a triangular shape. Dip each corner into the color and then carefully bend the corners aside and dip the middle section in color and let the color flow up into the paper. Now open up the square and lay it on the newspaper to dry (Figure 9-4b).

* Yet another way to fold the paper would be to make the pleated fan-fold mentioned earlier and then fold this entire fold again into a small version of a fan-fold, going back and forth until the entire paper is used and is in the shape of a little bundle (Figure 9-4c).

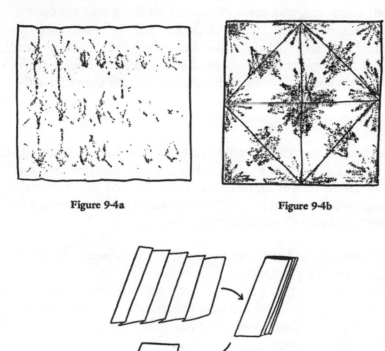

Figure 9-4a   Figure 9-4b

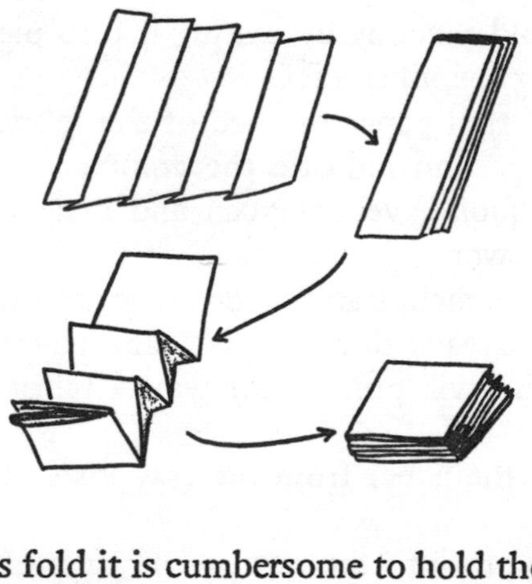

Figure 9-4c

* If during this fold it is cumbersome to hold the shape, an elastic band can be fastened around the paper to make it more stationary. The shape can then be dipped at each corner to produce yet another color design.

New Ways with Textiles

* If the paint is absorbed too quickly when dipping the paper, carefully squeeze some of the excess paint from the fold.
* When this lesson is being organized, it is a good idea to suggest that several squares and rectangles of paper be folded prior to the actual dipping. Be sure, however, that the folds are planned differently so that all the designs will be basically different.

5. Crayon Batik (Direct Color Method)

Batik is an ancient art craft that has its origin in southern Asia and Africa. There are two basic methods used in the original batik method: paste and wax resist. These are intricate and involved to do. We will not delve into the techniques here because they can be researched in any library, and they make interesting reading. However, the slow and tedious methods used by the batik craftsmen have been simplified for use in the classroom with the child-artist.

The technique described in this chapter will give the children a working opportunity to delve into the ancient art of batik.

> Materials: old sheets, pillowcases or new handkerchiefs (sizing removed); cold-water dyes; old scraps of crayons; old brushes; electric hotplate; muffin tins; water; waxed paper; newspaper; large discarded milk containers or cans; rubber gloves; vinegar; electric iron; solvent; trial paper; pencil.

* Prepare the old sheeting by tearing it into pieces about 18" X 18", or use a large handkerchief.
* On a piece of trial paper the size of the fabric, sketch a simple preliminary design and indicate the color areas. Yellow, orange, green, blue, turquoise, yellow-green and magenta are good color choices for batik work.
* With a soft-led pencil, transfer the design to the fabric.
* Pad the work area with newspaper, and cover the surface with waxed paper. This will prevent the waxed fabric from sticking to the newsprint.
* Next remove the paper from the crayons and break them into small pieces.
* Place the crayons into the sections of the muffin tins according to color.
* Then put the filled muffin tins in a container partially filled with water so it will not be directly over the heat of the electric plate.

* Heat the crayons until the muffin tins are filled with colored wax. (Be sure that the electric plate is kept at a low temperature and that there is always water in the container under the muffin tin.)
* Work in an area close to the melted wax.
* Start to paint the areas of design with the liquid wax, using the trial design as the basis for the work. Be sure as you apply the wax that it is penetrating through the fabric to the back. If it does not, plan to paint the reverse side with the wax when the front design is complete.
* If the wax starts to harden too rapidly, raise the temperature of the hot-plate so the hot wax is always fluid.
* When the entire design has been painted with wax and it is certain that the wax has seeped through to the back, set the fabric aside to cool.
* Now carefully pick up the fabric and start to crumple it back and forth, and then fashion it into a little ball.
* During this process much wax will break away from the fabric, so make sure there is ample newspaper underneath so the wax remains can be collected and reused at another time.
* Put on rubber gloves.
* Next, dip the ball of fabric into a strong, dark solution of dye. (Blue, green, black or brown are good dark dyes to use.)
* Open the ball and move the fabric around in the dye bath. The dye will penetrate the exposed area of the cracked cloth and the waxed areas will resist the dye color.
* Allow the fabric to remain in the dye bath for at least five minutes.
* Remove the cloth from the dye and place it on a pad of paper towels to absorb the excess dye.
* Now hang the designed fabric where it will dry quickly. (A line strung across the room is fine.)
* When the batik is dry, start to rub chips of wax from the fabric until a considerable amount has been removed.
* Remove the remaining crayon wax by either pressing the cloth between newspapers with a hot iron or by dipping the fabric into a solvent solution.
* The dye can easily be set into the fabric by immersing it in a solution of vinegar and then pressing the design with a hot iron.
* Be sure to clean the brushes and tins with solvent.
* The crackled Batik is now complete and ready to exhibit (Figure 9-5).

New Ways with Textiles

Figure 9-5

6. Painting with Yarn on Burlap

Painting with yarn and needle on a piece of fabric such as burlap is one of the most rewarding experiences a child can have.

Stitchery and *applique* work are not new forms of art work, but in recent years old rules about basic stitching have been replaced with new and original ways of placing stitches, cloth and color on a background. This allows creative ability to expand in such a tremendous way that the stamped and numbered needlework kits that had once been so prevalent have been abandoned by many for original stitchery work.

There are basic stitches that should be learned by the beginner so that the results will be more predictable, but after a little practice and skill, new stitching ideas will be created by the individual to make needlework an exciting hobby and pastime for future years.

> Materials: burlap; scissors; manila paper; pencil; white crayon; colored yarn; large-eyed needle; scrap fabric; newspaper; old sheeting; electric iron.

* Experiment on pieces of sheeting for practice in sewing the various stitches. They are:

a. Outline
b. Lazy Daisy
c. Running Stitch
d. Satin Stitch

e. Straight Stitch
f. Chain Stitch
g. Cross Stitch
h. Blanket Stitch
(Figure 9-6)

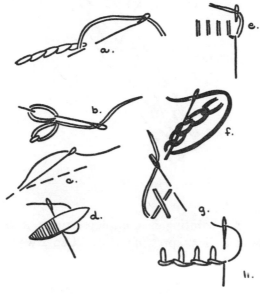

Figure 9-6

* It will help to have a well-thought-out plan prepared for the forthcoming project, so first draw a picture or design on a piece of paper the size of the burlap background.
* When the idea is drawn, transfer it to the center of a piece of burlap with a white crayon, leaving at least a two-inch margin all around the proposed sketch.
* Now thread the needle with the color yarn you desire to start with. Make a knot at the end of the thread and bring the needle up through the back of the burlap in the area you have designated for that particular yarn color. Begin to fill in areas of the sketch in the colors chosen. Always knot in the back.
* There are many stitches and variations that can be made while stitching, and soon it will be discovered that some areas can be outlined, others completely filled in, and still others shaded.
* While the stitching is in progress, try to keep the yarn from twisting.
* Try also to keep an even tension with the stitching so it will be as accurate and neat as possible.
* Pieces of fabric can be cut and added to parts of the picture by simply stitching around the additions. This is called applique work (Figure 9-7).

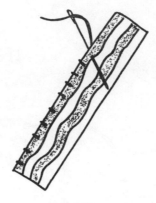

Figure 9-7

* When the fabric painting is complete, press it on a pad of newspapers under a clean pressing cloth. Use a warm iron and a dampened cloth.

* Mount or frame the completed work (Figure 9-8).

Figure 9-8

7. Felt-Tip Marker on Fabric

The felt-tip marker is steadily becoming a permanent part of the art program. It is easy and clean to use and its application is rapid and attractive. The marker makes broad, bold strokes, which can be varied immensely by pressure; and because it dries almost instantly, its lines are strong and decisive.

Since markers are so easy to manipulate, they can be managed by young children in place of pen and ink. Within just a few years, the color range in felt-tip markers has increased to include colors and shades of all types. However, this still remains an expensive medium.

Following is a technique that utilizes felt-tip marker on fabric. For classroom use, old sheeting remains an invaluable yet inexpensive source for the background of this wonderful project.

> Materials: old sheeting; scissors; felt-tip markers in a variety of colors; straight pins; crayons; trial paper; pencil; freezer or tissue paper; pad of newspaper.

* Tear the sheeting into pieces for the background.
* On trial paper the size of the sheeting, draw a picture or design. Color it with crayons to give color and line unity to the future fabric picture.
* When the student is satisfied with the picture, have it transferred to the sheeting with light-pencil sketch.
* Next cover the work area with a pad of newspaper, and place the fabric on top in preparation for the felt-tip marker work.
* Place and pin a piece of freezer or tissue paper over the fabric. If the sketch beneath is not visible, it will be necessary to go over the pencil lines to make them darker on the fabric (Figure 9-9).

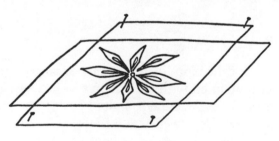

Figure 9-9

* Now, using the trial-colored sketch as an aid, begin to paint with the felt-tip markers on the freezer paper. The marker colors will seep through the freezer paper and penetrate the fabric, but the paper absorbs the excess color and prevents the marker from bleeding too freely on the fabric.
* Continue to paint with the markers until the entire picture is complete.
* If outlining is necessary, use a fine-line felt pen.
* Now remove the freezer paper and iron the fabric face-down on

New Ways with Textiles

a padding of newspaper. If a damp cloth is placed over the cloth before ironing, all wrinkles will be removed.

* Mount or frame the picture for best results (Figure 9-10).

Figure 9-10

8. Fabric Collage

A collage is a collection of fragments arranged in an artistic composition and mounted with an adhesive to heavyweight paper or cardboard. Because collages are not limited to any one medium, they can be extremely creative as well as fun to do.

The collage can be as simple or as complex as the creator would like to make it. Sometimes the materials are collected to depict a scene, face or just an interesting and exciting abstract design, which creates a nice arrangement of contrasting forms and colors. The collage suggested in the following section will be confined basically to the use of all types of fabric. However, other bonus materials can be added to the collage at the whim of the creator.

> Materials: stiff paper or cardboard at least 12″ X 18″ in size; an assortment of all types of fabrics (choose pieces with a variety of pattern, texture and feel); rubber cement; scissors; a potpourri of goodies such as yarn, thread, buttons, straws, feathers and ribbons.

* Discuss what a collage is, and possibly show examples of collages that were done by famous people, such as Arthur G. Dove's 1925 work called "Grandmother," and Picasso's 1914 work called "Bottle of Bass, Glass, Packet of Tobacco and Visiting Card."

* When the collage idea has been motivated, have the children begin by choosing pieces of fabric that are particularly interesting to them. Explain that the material should be chosen both for color and texture so that the unity of these will become a part of the design.

* Let the children play with the fabric to experience the feel and texture of each piece of cloth. Suggest that they shred and shape the fabric and spread the pieces out into appealing patterns.

* When the children have had an opportunity to discover some of the possibilities that the fabric offers, they can then begin to arrange the fabric into a design that is either suggestive of realism or a definite idea; and another possibility would be to simply make an abstract design, which is just pleasing to look at.

* A collage is a wonderful lesson because it can be changed often without damage to an original idea.

* When the composition is complete, it can be made permanent by picking up the fabric one piece at a time and adhering it to the background with rubber cement.

* The child will have to decide whether his arrangement is pleasing at this point. He may feel that other materials such as a piece of yarn or a string of buttons placed on the fabric

Figure 9-11

New Ways with Textiles

composition might help unify the idea. It is important for the adult to be available at this time to aid with a suggestion or a bit of advice.

* Mount the completed collage on a neutral background (Figure 9-11).

9. Fabric Treasure Box

Who has not, at some time or another, had at his disposal a very special box that was considered a hiding place for special treasures? Here is an idea, using fabric, which utilizes the collage technique with a craft idea that will produce a very special product.

Materials: a sturdy box with a lid (shoe boxes are excellent); an assortment of all kinds of fabric; scissors; rubber cement.

* In another lesson the basic concept of a collage was mentioned, so the collage idea will not be new to the children.
* Prior to the lesson, suggest that the children bring to class their own cache of cloth and the box needed for the project.
* Most often the children will keep the pieces of fabric that they are particularly fond of and put the remaining material in a community-type box for further use by themselves or by their peers.

Figure 9-12

* The fabric pieces are then cut into shapes and slowly glued to the box in an attractive arrangement.
* Suggest that the fabric be fastened as flat as possible to prevent an air bubble or buckle in the cloth. It is also an excellent idea to place the fabric so it is slightly overlapping the piece that has been put on the time before.
* Continue to add the patches of color until the entire box is covered with a patchwork design. Be sure that one color texture is not placed together in any one place.
* When both the box and the lid are covered with the fabric, the shoe box becomes a wonderful artistic treasure (Figure 9-12).

New Ways with Textiles

10

Plaster, Styrofoam and Wax—
Space-Age Projects

With the introduction of new ideas into the art curriculum, new and varied materials have come into use. Just a few years ago, plaster, Styrofoam and wax were rarely used as art media in the classroom. However, the present generation of students is no longer satisfied with the basics in art media — crayon, paint and paper cutting; they are in search of new and adventuresome materials, which we must continually search for and offer if our role as art educators is to be fulfilled.

Plaster and wax have been used by the artist for centuries in sculpting, fresco and mold work, and these materials are now emerging in new techniques that can be used by the child-artist. Although these materials are not prohibitively expensive, they can put a strain on the art budget if used in great quantities. Styrofoam, however, is an item that is readily available because of its abundant use in packaging: it can be found in large-size pieces used for packaging large items, and in the smaller sizes used for packaging food items such as meat and eggs. Also, Styrofoam has recently begun to replace excelsior and shredded paper and, as a result, we get all sorts of delightful little shapes in various colors. (Doughnut, shell, peanut and spaghetti shapes are a few of the descriptive names that have been coined by children.)

Start saving all kinds of new materials for use in the art program. With the knowledge that "different" materials will be the start of new and challenging art projects, the children will be a ready and enthusiastic source of these new materials.

A. HOW TO USE PLASTER, STYROFOAM AND WAX

Although not all the suggestions mentioned in this chapter are adaptable to all classes, the techniques can be altered or expanded to make them suitable to almost any age group.

1. Plaster Sculpting

Sculpting in plaster is a wonderful experience for children. Unlike wood or stone, the plaster has a semi-hard finish, which makes it easy to carve with the simplest of tools.

Be sure when working with plaster that all precautions are observed for clean-up. Plaster must always be discarded into a refuse can; it must not come in contact with the sink or drain in any way. When mixing the plaster, always add the plaster to the water and, if possible, mix each batch in small quantities in disposable cans or milk cartons. Hands are the best mixing tool, but a stick or old ruler will also do. The addition of a small quantity of flour, borax or vinegar will slow down the setting time of plaster. Salt or warm water will speed the setting time.

The chemical action that takes place during the mixing process will cause the mixture to radiate a slight heat. Children should be advised of this in advance so they won't be unnecessarily alarmed.

> Materials: plaster of Paris; water; container such as a large discarded can for mixing; discarded quart and pint milk cartons for molds; tools, such as nail files, old kitchen knives or scissors; tempera paint; sandpaper.

* Fill the container approximately 2/3 full with water. Carefully sift the plaster steadily into the water until a mound of plaster is just above the water line. (Placing plaster into water will eliminate excess bubbles from forming in the completed mold.)
* Next, gently stir the plaster and water with the hands or an old ruler until the consistency appears even throughout the mixture.
* If color is desired instead of stark-white plaster, add some tempera paint at this point by swirling it into the plaster mold while it is hardening.

Plaster, Styrofoam and Wax—Space-Age Projects

* Tap the bottom of the container in order to take out any remaining air bubbles.
* Now let the plaster set overnight.
* When ready to sculpt, strip the container away from the mold and begin to work in the form. Use any of the tools mentioned to do the sculpting.
* It is best to work with the block of plaster if there is a pre-planned idea or sketch of what the four sides, top and bottom, of the completed sculpture will look like. However, the sculptor can depart from this whenever he chooses.
* If a piece of plaster breaks away from the form, a piece can sometimes be added. To do this, soak the form with the broken area submerged in water. When it is thoroughly wet, remove it from the water and add the new plaster. The rule here is to always apply wet to wet when patching plaster.
* When the work is complete, sand it so it will be smooth.
* At this point the shape can remain in this form or be attached to a wood base with glue (Figure 10-1).

Figure 10-1

2. Plaster Blob Jewelry

Teachers are always searching for an inexpensive craft-gift for an art activity. Here is an inexpensive idea that is very simple to do, and impressive results are attained for a little bit of effort.

Materials: plaster of Paris; waxed paper or silver foil; old ruler; discarded large milk carton or cans; watercolors; brushes; water;

newspaper; clear nail lacquer; flat-back pins; medical cotton; duco cement; emory board.

* Cover the work area with newspaper.
* Mix the plaster. Do this by filling a container half full with water. Then gradually sift the plaster of Paris into the water until the mixture is the consistency of cream.
* Now carefully begin to pour the plaster in blobs on the waxed paper or silver foil. The plaster will spread slightly, so leave enough space in between. As the plaster is being poured, try to make the shapes into unusual forms. Pull the plaster as it is being poured to make shapes long and thin, free form, circular, or dough-nut-shaped with a hole in the middle (Figure 10-2a).

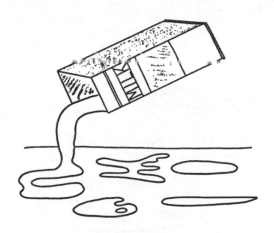

Figure 10-2a

* Pour fast or the plaster will dry in the container before all the shapes are completed.
* When the plaster has all been used or when it has become too dry to use, discard what is left along with the carton.
* Now let the plaster pieces dry thoroughly.
* Peel the dried plaster pieces carefully from the paper or foil, and, with an emory board, smooth out any rough edges or edges that might appear too fragile. The plaster is very delicate, so handle it with a great deal of care.
* Paint the plaster blobs with watercolors and fine-tipped brushes. Color them with designs of nature, geometric patterns or just color shapes that are pleasing to look at.

Plaster, Styrofoam and Wax—Space-Age Projects

* Coat each pin with several layers of clear nail lacquer. The finish made with the lacquer is extremely shiny and gives the pin a very professional look.
* Remember also to coat the back with at least one coat of lacquer so the white chalk of the plaster won't come off on someone's clothing.
* Next, glue a flat-back pin onto the back of the blob with the duco cement. Put a fine hair of cotton fiber in the cement before the pin is attached. A chemical reaction results between the cotton fiber, glue and the plaster, so the pin back remains intact indefinitely.
* When the project is complete, no two pins will be the same. This in itself lends to the beauty of a lesson that is purely creative (Figure 10-2b).

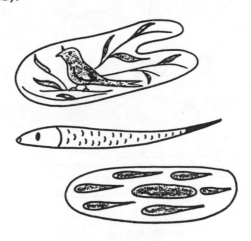

Figure 10-2b

3. Plaster Prints

Plaster, a versatile medium, can be used in a project that calls for two basic steps. It can be used as a base for graphic, and also as a wonderful carving experience.

Materials: plaster of Paris; water; container such as a large can or milk carton for mixing purposes; sturdy, flat cardboard box; sharp tools such as old kitchen knives, scissors, nail file, compass point; printing ink or thick tempera; brayer; trial paper; pencil; newsprint paper, tissue or lightweight paper.

* First, mix the plaster and water in the mixing container until the plaster is the consistency of heavy cream.
* Now carefully pour the mixture into the flat cardboard box and level the surface with a ruler so it is smooth.
* Tap the bottom of the box on the working surface to remove excess air bubbles.
* Now put the plaster aside to set for several hours or overnight.
* When the plaster is thoroughly dry, remove it from the cardboard box.
* Next, draw a sketch on a piece of paper the size of the plaster mold.
* When the idea is pleasing, transfer it to the smooth side of the plaster mold with pencil.
* Next, scratch, cut out, gouge and scrape portions of the design from the surface of the plaster. This is not difficult because the plaster is a semi-hard material.
* Carve the plaster so the indentations are deep enough to form true textural patterns and the original pencil sketch becomes a relief picture.
* Now put some colored ink or thick tempera paint on the aluminum foil and run the brayer through it several times to pick up the color.
* Brayer the color on the plaster relief plate.
* Next, quickly take a piece of newsprint or other lightweight paper and center it on the plaster mold.
* Press over the paper firmly with the hand until all areas of the paper have been completely rubbed.
* Now lift the paper, and there is a print from the plaster on it (Figure 10-3).

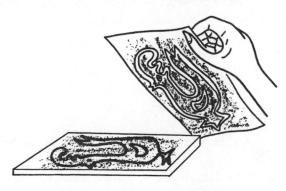

Figure 10-3

* If the first print shows a fault in the basic design, wipe off the excess color and recarve the areas to be changed.
* Re-ink the plaster plate before each print for the best results. Any number of prints can be lifted from a plaster plate.

NOTE: The carved plaster plate is handsome to display after its use as a printing plate has been exhausted.

4. Sand Casting

The best place to do a sand-casting project is at the beach. However, when this opportunity does not afford itself, the next-best thing to do is to bring the beach sand to the classroom for the project. The sand can be reused over and over again, and it offers a wonderful opportunity to sand sculpt in a most creative and inexpensive way.

> Materials: a sturdy, flat cardboard box about 12" X 18"; enough sand to fill the box half way up its side; plaster of Paris; large discarded cans or milk cartons; water; nature's treasures: shells, pretty stones, pieces of wood; hairpin or a paper clip.

* Discuss and demonstrate the procedure for making and shaping the hole for the mold, setting in the treasure objects, mixing and pouring the plaster of Paris and, finally, adding the hairpin or paper clip for future hanging, before the children actually do their own work.
* Now follow the procedure with the group assisting when necessary.
* First, moisten the sand with water and fill a flat cardboard box half way up the side with the sand. (Be sure that the sand is not too wet or the box will break.)
* Carefully make a shallow hole in the sand and shape the base-relief mold. If the shape is not satisfactory after the first attempt, shape and develop it again.
* Now place the stones and shells in position to give the sculpture a little variety in color.
* Then carefully mix the plaster and water to a heavy-cream consistency.
* Gently pour the mixture into the base-relief so the shapes will not be jostled (Figure 10-4a).

* Fill the box to the top with the plaster mixture.
* Before the plaster sets, add the hairpin or clip to the plaster back so the shape can be hung at a future time. If the plaster mold appears too huge or heavy for hanging, either add another clip or sink a piece of wood into the plaster and later a base can be screwed into this.
* Let the plaster set overnight, and then remove the box by peeling away the sides to separate the plaster relief from its bed in the sand. Notice that the plaster sculpture is just the reverse of the original mold (Figure 10-4b).

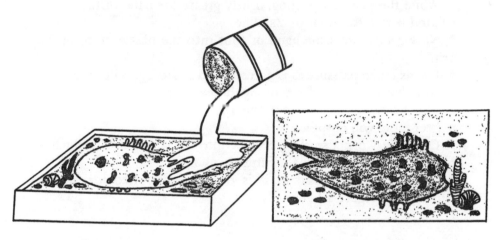

Figure 10-4a   Figure 10-4b

* Much sand will remain on the plaster cast. This somewhat enhances the beauty of the piece. However, if it appears that there is too much sand, brush it off with a stiff brush of some sort. (A toothbrush is great!)
* The natural state of the sand sculpture is most appealing to the eye, but color can be added to the sculpture with tempera paint if so desired.

5. Hand and Foot Prints

A replica of a child's hand or foot print is a wonderful treat for parents. Although not completely creative in nature, its production deserves merit because it records personal history.

Plaster, Styrofoam and Wax—Space-Age Projects

Materials: large aluminum pie tins; Vaseline; plaster of Paris; water; discarded large cans or milk cartons; paint; brushes; block of wood; eye screws.

* Coat the pie tin with a thin layer of Vaseline.
* Lay a small block of wood at the bottom of the tin.
* Mix the plaster of Paris until it is the consistency of heavy cream.
* Carefully pour the mixture into the aluminum pie tin. Make sure the wood block remains intact at the bottom of the tin (Figure 10-5a).
* While the plaster is setting, lightly grease the hand or foot to be printed with a thin coat of Vaseline.
* Now gently press the hand or foot into the plaster to form the print.
* Use as much pressure as is necessary to make a good print.
* Now let the plaster dry thoroughly overnight.
* The next day, gently tap the foil pan on the back and the plaster mold will drop out.
* Carefully work a small eye screw into the wood block, which is plaster-imbedded. This is for future hanging.
* The print can remain as it is or can be painted for further adornment (Figure 10-5b).

Figure 10-5a   Figure 10-5b

6. Nature Collage

Preserving nature is a wonderful way to record beauty. This task is often quite difficult because of the heavy weight of the materials involved. Stones, shells, nuts and pieces of wood are difficult to fasten to a background; but with the aid of a thin plaster layer, this can be done quite efficiently, and the beauty of the material remains.

> Materials: plaster of Paris; flour; sturdy, flat cardboard box; water; a variety of nature's treasures; can for mixing plaster; screws; wood block; gesso; brushes.

* Prior to the lesson, suggest that the students collect an assortment of nature's treasures. They can be shells, stones, pine cones, pieces of wood, seeds, bark, etc.
* On the designated day, assemble the treasures into an arrangement that is interesting and will show the pieces to their best advantage. Placing shapes in plaster is final, so be sure that the arrangement made is one that will always be pleasant to look at.
* Now mix the plaster of Paris and water to the consistency of heavy cream. Add just a bit of flour to slow down the drying time, so the pieces can be placed in the wet plaster before it hardens and sets.
* Place a small cube of wood about ½" X 1" in the bottom of the box for the future base.
* Now pour the mixture very slowly and carefully into the box. Make sure the wood remains intact at the bottom of the box.
* Fill the box about half full with the plaster.
* Then quickly transfer the shapes that were earlier assembled at the side into the plaster. Press the pieces into the mixture but be sure they are not pushed in too far (Figure 10-6a).

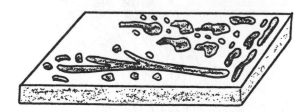

Figure 10-6a

* Continue to add the treasures to the plaster until the completed work is assembled into a beautiful, permanent nature collage.
* Now let the work dry overnight.
* The next step is to remove the mold from the box. This can be done quite easily by cutting the box at the corners and stripping it

away from the plaster. The plaster is fragile, so this must be done very cautiously.

* Next, hold the plaster cast upright in position and carefully attach the eye screw to the block of wood, which was first imbedded in the plaster. When this is accomplished, the collage is ready for display (Figure 10-6b).

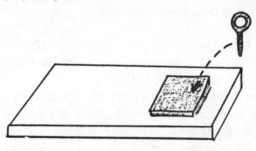

Figure 10-6b

Added Suggestion

* Perishable items such as weeds, thistles, different wild straws and grasses can also be embedded in plaster.
* This can be done most effectively if they are first dried for a short period of time before they are placed into the plaster.
* When the materials are dry, arrange them on a piece of cardboard and have them ready to place in the plaster.

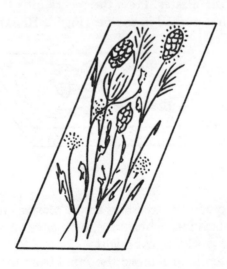

Figure 10-6c

* Mix the plaster and pour it into the box as suggested previously. (Be sure not to forget the block of wood at the bottom of the box, or you will not be able to hang the cast.)

* When the plaster is poured, lay the dried weeds into the plaster and set the arrangement aside to dry overnight.

* Remove the mold from the box.

* Add an eerie, pale look to the weed arrangement by painting over areas of the collage with a thin coat of gesso. The weeds will retain their charm indefinitely (Figure 10-6c).

7. Paint on Plaster

Plaster is an absorbent material and, when used for a painted background, it becomes an unusual medium. Painting on plaster is not a new idea; the early frescos used this technique. Also, the plaster is a unique background to use because it cannot be purchased like a canvas. It has to be custom-made by the artist.

Materials: flat cardboard box (stocking or glove boxes are wonderful); patching plaster; large can; water; old ruler; tempera paints; brushes; newspaper; trial paper; pencil.

* Cover the work area with newspaper.

* Mix the plaster just thick enough to be poured.

* Then carefully pour the plaster into the boxes, and level the surface with a ruler.

* Hit the bottom of the box on the working surface to disperse any miscellaneous air bubbles.

* Before the plaster sets, place a paper clip or bent wire in the back of the mold for future hanging.

* Allow the plaster to set overnight. Then remove the plaster board from the cardboard box. This can be done easily by just tearing away the box.

* Now make a trial sketch of the design or picture you care to paint on a piece of paper the size of the plaster board.

* Transfer the sketch to the plaster board with a light pencil.

* Start to apply the paint to the board, but apply it in a "mock-fresco" method of painting, one color wash at a time. The more applications of washes, the deeper the color. (The plaster acts like a sponge. As the color is applied, it seeps deep into the plaster.)

* Pure white is produced by scratching away the surface to reveal the plaster underneath.

* The plaster painting offers various possibilities, all depending upon the creativity of the child. How much or how little is done on a particular work depends upon the child-artist (Figure 10-7).

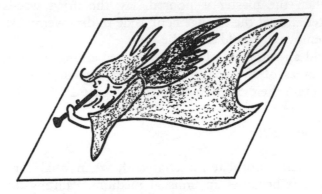

Figure 10-7

8. Styrofoam Construction

Styrofoam is usually available just for the asking. It is so readily available that just a suggestion of "We need Styrofoam" will be all that is needed to fill the classroom with an abundance of this wonderful material. It is a great art material for use by children because it is lightweight, can be cut easily and can be glued and painted without difficulty. It is especially good for use in construction work, but its possibilities are endless.

Materials: Styrofoam; serrated knives†; white glue; straight-pins; wire coat hangers; tempera paints; liquid soap; brushes; coping saws; yarn; colored toothpicks.

* When making a Styrofoam construction it is probably most advisable to set out the stock of Styrofoam and let the children build their constructions as they go along.
* Each child can start with a knife brought from home and a slab of Styrofoam that he can cut into the shapes desired.
* If possible, it is excellent to have at least five coping saws available for cutting larger pieces of foam that cannot be manipulated with the serrated knives.

---

† A good serrated edge for cutting foam is the cutting edge of a used waxpaper or aluminum-foil container.

* Cut the hangers into rods to be used as the supports for pieces that will not stand up by themselves.

* When the pieces are cut, the shapes can be combined with glue, pins or rods to join the shapes together.

* Excess glue will melt the foam, so use the glue sparingly and depend mainly upon the pins and the wire rods for stability in the construction. Two pieces can be glued and pinned together until the glue dries, and then if the spot is not a crucial one, the pins can be removed. Use a bit of flour mixed with the white glue if it does not stick readily.

* The constructions do not have to resemble anything realistic. They can be forms constructed for pure beauty of height and shape (Figure 10-8).

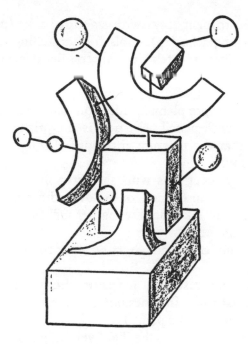

Figure 10-8

* For color, string, colored toothpicks and paint can be added to the construction. (If the tempera paint will not cover the foam readily, add a bit of liquid soap to the paint and try again.)

* The final projects are remarkable to behold. They perfectly reflect the student-artist's creativity and ingenuity using simple, inexpensive materials.

Plaster, Styrofoam and Wax—Space-Age Projects

9. Styrofoam Prints

Here is another wonderful way to use Styrofoam, this time, not as a construction medium, but as a plate for a graphic. Again, it is an excellent medium because it can be obtained at no cost and its use eliminates the tedious cutting of wood and linoleum in the process of making a graphic.

Because the foam is sturdy and yet soft it can be scratched and gouged out with a pair of scissors or a simple nail. However, it can also be melted away in a fine line by using the ink from felt-tip markers, so an impression can be placed on the plate in any individual number of ways or a combination of ways.

> Materials: Styrofoam trays with smooth backs (obtained from meat and fruit packaging); tools for scratching, such as nails, scissors, nail files; old felt-tip markers; lightweight paper, such as newsprint or colored tissue.

* Draw a simple pre-planned idea on the smooth side of a styrofoam tray with pencil. The tray is the printing plate. It will be discovered that the pressure of the pencil will leave a beginning gouge on the tray.
* Now either go over this with a sharp-pointed instrument, to make the incised line deeper, or go over the pencil line with a felt-tip marker. The ink from the marker will further eat away the line formed by the pencil.
* If the line is not deep enough, cut deeper for a good impression (Figure 10-9a).
* Next, using the easel brush, paint the printing plate with tempera paint. (If the paint does not stick, remember to add a few drops of liquid soap to the paint.)
* Now center a piece of the lightweight paper over the tray (printing plate), and carefully rub the surface with the side of your hand.
* Remove the paper from the printing plate and you will discover a fine-line print (Figure 10-9b).
* The Styrofoam tray is quite sturdy, and many prints can be made from it.
* Another interesting effect is obtained by printing the plate in an assortment of colors. The suggestions are given . . .experiment!

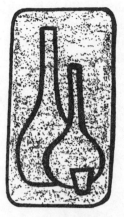

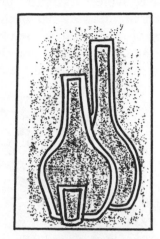

Figure 10-9a   **Figure 10-9b**

10. Styrofoam Mosaics

Styrofoam trays can be cut so easily with a pair of scissors that they become much sought-after items for the tesserae in a mosaic.

> Materials: Styrofoam trays; scissors; 9″ X 12″ cardboard base; white glue; tempera paint; trial sketch paper; pencil; brushes; liquid soap; polymer medium.

* First, coat both sides of the cardboard with polymer medium to seal it so it will not have a tendency to warp.
* Paint the trays on the smooth side with solid colors of tempera paint. (If the paint does not adhere to the Styrofoam, remember to add a few drops of liquid soap to it.) Use at least five different colors of paint so there will be a variety of different colors of tesserae.
* Set the trays aside to dry.
* Now make a simple sketch of some object for the mosaic you plan to do.
* Redraw the idea lightly on cardboard.
* Next, cut the dried trays into shapes no larger than pieces of small tile about ¾″ in size. Do not limit the shapes to rectangles or squares. Try cutting free-form shapes, which will add interest to the completed mosaic.
* Start to fit the colored pieces into the design that was drawn.

* Glue each piece into place on the cardboard.

* When the drawing has been completely filled in with tesserae, the Styrofoam mosaic is complete (Figure 10-10).

* The mosaic may not need to be framed, but it can be by adding thin, narrow strips around the edges for a nice finish.

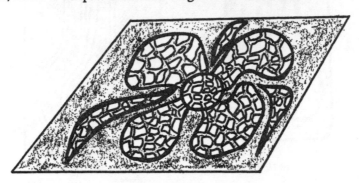

Figure 10-10

11. Styrofoam Egg Cartons

Materials: Styrofoam egg cartons; scissors; tempera paint; brushes; fancy buttons; beads; ribbons; pipe cleaners; rick-rack; white glue.

* The egg cartons almost speak for themselves. They can be kept intact, painted and decorated with sequins, buttons, ribbons and rick-rack to make a special treasure box (Figure 10-11a).

* A carton can be cut and used for junk printing (Figure 10-11b).

* Colored cartons can be cut into sections and used as flowers. All that is needed is a pipe-cleaner stem and a clay base in which to stand the flowers (Figure 10-11c).

* Parts of the cartons can be assembled, glued and painted to form little animals or people (Figure 10-11d).

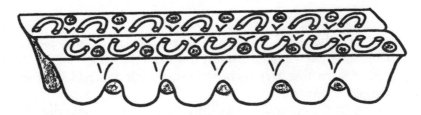

Figure 10-11a

* Another possibility would be to cut the pieces and add them either to a paper collage or in an assemblage as possible eyes and nose for part of a paper sculpture or a puppet (Figure 10-11e).

* No matter how the carton is used it proves to be an invaluable asset to the art in a classroom.

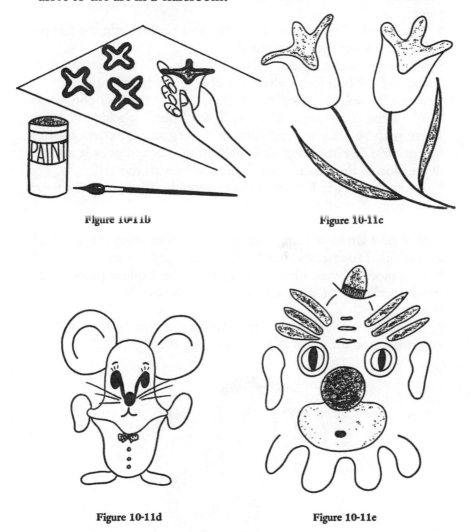

Figure 10-11b

Figure 10-11c

Figure 10-11d

Figure 10-11e

12. Wax Sculpture

Wax sculpting is another wonderful sculpting exercise. It is especially good to use with children because the margin of error is so much less than it is with plaster or wood sculpting.

Materials: old wax candles; bits of colored crayon; discarded milk cartons; hotplate; large cans; flat pan; water; scissors; kitchen knives; nail files; medium-weight sandpaper.

* Remove the wicks from the candles and break the candles into pieces.
* Put the candle pieces into the can and place this in the flat pan containing water over the hotplate.
* Melt the candle pieces. Always watch this process carefully. Make sure the hotplate is always kept at a low temperature.
* When the wax is melted, pour it slowly into the milk containers.
* When the container is filled with wax, place it aside to harden. There may be a slight depression in the center of the wax form. If this occurs, do not be alarmed, melt more wax and pour it into the depression so the wax is at the same level across the top.
* Allow the wax to harden at least overnight. Then strip the paper mold away from it and sculpting can begin.
* Use the tools mentioned for the carving.
* It is best when working with wax to sculpt freely. Have a basic idea in mind to attempt, but try to avoid a paper plan.
* If a piece of wax breaks away, heat the broken piece with a small candle flame and attach it quickly to the area where it belongs.
* When the work is complete, smooth the wax surface with the sandpaper and then buff it with a soft rag (Figure 10-12).

Figure 10-12

13. Free-Form Wax Shapes

Here is an interesting way to use up old candles. The technique used is quite bizarre.

> Materials: old candles with wicks removed; crayons; newspaper; pail of water; all sorts of small containers, such as jar lids, foil cups, foil pans, small glasses, cut-down milk containers.

* Cover the work area with newspaper.
* Break the candles into pieces and melt them in a large can over the hotplate.
* Make sure the can is only partially filled with wax, and that the hotplate is kept at a low temperature.
* Pour the melted wax carefully into a little container that you have ready, and with both hands plunge the container boldly into the cold water.
* Push the container all the way to the bottom of the pail.
* The wax begins to harden with its first contact with the cold water, and as it hardens it mysteriously forms beautiful shapes from the holding container to the surface of the water in the pail.
* Hold the shape in the water for a few seconds and, when the wax is firmly set, carefully remove the container and wax from the water.

Figure 10-13

Plaster, Styrofoam and Wax—Space-Age Projects

Variations

* Twist the wax creation as it is plunged into the water and see the unusual effect this gives the shape.

* Add two or more colors of hot wax to the containers and see how the colors combine to form interesting patterns.

* Another possibility is to add a piece of dried material, such as a weed or grass, to the wax just before it is submerged into the water. Notice how the wax climbs the stalk and is deposited on the various areas of it.

* No matter what the method, the wax form will take on shapes that are incredibly unique. No two will ever be exactly the same (Figure 10-13). The work and the final pieces are interesting to do and see. However, the wax is extremely fragile, so care must be taken in their preservation.

14. Sand-Casted Candles

Here is another use for the sand that we used in the plaster-of-Paris *sand casting*.

> Materials: paraffin or used white candles (with the wicks removed); old crayons; hotplate; pail or large, sturdy boxes of sand; stick or pencil; large can for melting wax; water.

* Place the sand in a container. A pail or sturdy box is fine.

* Moisten but do not soak the sand with water.

* Now scoop out a small hole the size you would like the candle to be.

* With a stick or pencil, pierce the walls of the hole just dug several times in different areas. This will give the candle little feet, which will help the candle stand up.

* Break up the old candles into small pieces and melt them over the hotplate in the large can. (Save the wicks that were removed from the old candles.)

* Add colored crayons to the wax to give the candles the color desired.

* Now tie one of the wicks around the center of a long stick and lay it over the hole for the proposed candle.

* The wick should extend all the way down the hole that was prepared.

* Now slowly pour the wax into the sand mold. Make sure the wick hangs in the middle of the wax shape.
* If the wax does not fill the hole, melt more wax and pour it carefully over the first wax.
* Set the candle aside to harden completely.
* When it is thoroughly set, cut the wick away from the stick and gently lift the candle away from the sand mold.
* Carefully wipe away the excess sand.
* The candle can remain in this form with the layer of light sand encrusted around the outside of the colored candle (Figure 10-14). Or, the entire candle can be redipped in another color wax. This is done by holding the wick-top and dipping the entire wax and sand form into a batch of hot wax. The new wax color will adhere to the sand and candle, but the process must be done rapidly or the original candle will melt.

Figure 10-14

Plaster, Styrofoam and Wax—Space-Age Projects

11

Hints, Suggestions and Recipes

The primary purpose of this book is to offer to the art novice techniques and suggestions for the use of art materials in the classroom, and I feel that the book would not be fulfilling its purpose if it did not contain a few suggestions to help the teacher expedite the planning of and preparation for the art lesson. These suggestions are not meant to replace traditional art procedures and materials; rather, they are an attempt to provide concrete help, stimulation and excitement to what might otherwise be a routine art program.

A. HINTS AND SUGGESTIONS

The most valuable aid in helping to set up the classroom for a workable art program would be to outline those materials that should be available in the classroom. The ready availability of these materials and a knowledge of their use should contribute greatly to any art lesson.

CRAYONS — new ones, and a box of assorted scrap pieces.

CONSTRUCTION PAPER — all sizes, colors and a scrap box of assorted paper, which might include wallpaper, grass papers, metallic paper, flourescent paper, rice paper, textured paper.

SCISSORS — for each child and large shears for the teacher (for heavy paper and textile cutting).

RUBBER CEMENT — PASTE — GLUE

MANILA PAPER — at least 12″ X 18″ in size.

WHITE PAPER — at least 12" X 18" in size.

TEMPERA PAINT — the primary colors plus an assortment of other colors.

BRUSHES — a variety of sizes for large, free work and small, precise work.

STAPLER

TAPE — masking and Scotch tape.

STRING — YARN — CORD — in an assortment of colors.

STRAIGHT PINS — NEEDLES — with large eyes.

FELT-TIP MARKERS — assorted colors.

"GOODIE BOX" — containing buttons, ribbons, lace, wire, beads, colored glass, doilies, straws, sequins, etc.

FABRIC BOX — assortment of scrap fabrics such as burlap, satins, cottons, velvet, mesh, net, synthetics, upholstery fabric, fake fur, simulated leather.

WOOD BOX — scraps of all kinds of wood in an assortment of sizes, plus hammer and nails.

SUPPLY OF NEWSPAPERS AND RAGS.

B. HELPFUL HINTS PERTAINING TO ART MATERIALS

The realm of art materials is vast. What I will attempt to do is list the most popular art media or tools and try to offer helpful advice about their use.

1. Paint

* Always clean tops of screw-edge, liquid paint jars after each use. The application of Vaseline on the rim will prevent jar tops from sticking and a piece of plastic wrap over the rim will further serve this purpose.
* If the top of the jar is difficult to remove, hit the lid top, flat side down, on the floor.
* Prevent tempera from drying out by floating water on top of the paint.

* Always thin paint with water before use. Thick paint, when dry, chips off readily.
* Keep watercolor boxes clean and replace colors when necessary.
* A little liquid starch added to tempera paint will keep it from running or dripping.
* If an easel is unavailable, manila or easel paper can be clipped with a spring-type clothespin or secretarial clip to a large, stiff piece of cardboard and leaned against a table or wall for painting.
* Liquid starch can be added to thick tempera and used for finger painting.
* Add liquid or powdered soap to tempera or rub your brush on soap before painting when you have a difficult surface to cover, such as crayon, glass, or wax cartons.
* If a palatte is needed for painting, use lids of jars, aluminum pie plates, or heavy aluminum foil with the sides folded up and shaped into a form for holding the paint.
* Any number of items can hold small portions of tempera paint. Have you tried plastic egg cartons, plastic or paper cups, small waxed milk cartons or aluminum trays? They are all plentiful and can be discarded without washing.
* A discarded spray bottle filled with water or a large sponge are excellent for wetting paper when doing a finger painting, or as a wash for a watercolor painting.
* If paint doesn't come in squeeze bottles, an old, large spoon is wonderful for scooping paint from the bottle.
* Old rulers are excellent for stirring paint.
* When painting on cloth, rub the brush over soap before applying the paint. The soap prevents the paint from spreading or fanning on the cloth.
* When painting with a spray can, always make sure that the arrow is pointed in the proper direction before adding the pressure.
* Tape or pin a spray project to the inside of a large carton. This becomes a makeshift spray box, and there will not be a difficult clean-up job.
* Cover your work area with newspaper whenever painting. This aids in clean-up afterwards.

2. Familiarize Your Students with the Use of Color.

* Red, yellow and blue are the primary colors. They cannot be made; you must have them.
* Orange, purple and green are the secondary colors. They can be made.

Red plus yellow makes orange.
Red plus blue makes purple.
Blue plus yellow makes green.
* Brown is a Tertiary Color. It is made by the combination of three colors: the primary colors, red, yellow and blue.
* Black and White are not colors. They are shades. To make a light color or shade of a color start with white and add small amounts of the base color until the color desired is obtained.
* To darken a color add minute quantities of black to the base color until the color desired is obtained.
* To cool a color add blue to the base color.
* To warm a color add yellow to the base color.

No matter what the medium — tempera, watercolors, oil or acrylics — the color principles remain the same.

3. Brushes

* Clean tempera and watercolor brushes with water after each use.
* Clean brushes used with polymer with water and keep them in water during the work process.
* Clean brushes used with permanent paint, such as oils and enamels, with turpentine; clean lacquers and shellac with alcohol.
* An easy way to store brushes is with the brush side up in a can or jar. Place a paper towel at the bottom of the container to absorb any moisture that might be on the brush handle after washing.
* When cleaning brushes, always form a point with the bristles so they will dry in this form and be ready for future use.
* Store camel-hair brushes flat in a container that is protected by moth flakes.
* Experiment with improvised tools when using paint. Instead of brushes, try using cut-up sponges, string, rags, pieces of Styrofoam, straws, sticks, feathers, Q-Tips and brayers.
* Put paint into empty roll-on or spray bottles. Apply the paint with these tools.
* Fill empty plastic squeeze bottles with paint. Dribble and drop paint from the bottles onto the working surface. If the paint pours too freely, add liquid starch to the tempera paint. It will become thick enough to control while pouring.
* Always work gently with brushes. Do not scrub them into paint.
* Do not leave brushes bristle side down in paint.

Hints, Suggestions and Recipes

4. Adhesives

* White school paste is not waterproof. Plastic cement, duco cement and rubber cement are waterproof.
* Metallic paper will not adhere to a background with white paste. Use rubber cement.
* Acrylics can be used as an adhesive and for providing rich glazes to the surface of a product.
* Rubber cement is excellent for use in *resist* projects. Always keep the can of cement securely fastened when not in use. Refill the cans periodically.
* Polymer acts as a *sealer,* and can be used to coat both sides of a material such as cardboard to prevent it from warping.
* Use epoxy cement to adhere heavy objects to a background surface.
* Projects for the outdoors must be joined with a waterproof adhesive if an adhesive is the method you are using.
* A simple homemade adhesive can be prepared by mixing flour and water.
* Undiluted liquid starch also makes a fine adhesive.
* Styrofoam will adhere to a surface if white glue is mixed with a little flour and used as the adhesive. When dry, the rough edges can be smoothed with sandpaper.
* If polymer medium is unavailable, substitute four parts of Elmer's glue with one part water and use this. It will not dry as shiny, however.
* Elmer's glue thickened with flour makes a good substitute for wallpaper paste when doing papier mache.
* Float water on top of white school paste to keep it from drying out.
* Always clean up excess glue or paste smears as soon as they occur. A wet paper towel somewhere in the working area aids in keeping sticky fingers clean.
* If a glue pot does not have its own applicator, use an old paint brush for spreading the glue. Remove the glue with soap and warm water or, if using rubber cement, use thinner to clean the brush.

5. Crayons

* Try to order crayons unwrapped. They can be used in more ways with the wrapping removed.

* Have crayons stored in individual sturdy boxes — one set per child.
* Save small scrap crayons in a community crayon box.
* Order some extra black and white crayons; they are usually the first to go.
* If possible, order special crayons, such as gold and silver or the new flourescent crayons.
* Experiment with crayons. Use them in mosaics, melted, chipped, etched, and with other materials. Use them on different surfaces: sandpaper, wood, stone, fabrics, different papers.
* Make new crayons by melting scraps of different colors in a can over low heat. Pour the wax into small fruit-juice cans. When the wax cools, the children will have new and different-colored crayons with which to work. The size of the homemade crayon will fascinate them.
* Crayons are great to bring along on field trips. They are easy to carry and will not spill like paint.

6. Paper

* Magazine pages and shelf paper are great substitutes when finger-paint paper is required for a project.
* A good supply of newspaper is always good to have in the classroom. Use them for drawing and painting as well as for clean-up.
* Paper browns quickly at the edges and cracks when it is old. Rotate the paper supply by putting the new paper under the old when a new order arrives.
* Cut paper into a variety of sizes so that just the right size is always available for use.
* Teach children to cut from corners when they are cutting small objects from a piece of paper. This avoids waste. Also, have children get into the habit of saving scraps of paper that can be used for other projects.
* Arrange colored paper in groups of the same color.
* Poster paper, unless it is the "fadeless" variety, will discolor rapidly when exposed to sunlight. Consider the use of colored tissue paper instead. It seems to keep its color longer in sunlight.
* Crepe and tissue paper make excellent dye color. Wet them and place them on dry, solid-colored paper. The dye will transfer to the dry paper.
* When doing papier-mache work, tear the paper strips. When the

mache is dry, the paper seams will not show readily.

* Use a variety of different paper textures for displaying projects. Wallpaper, metallic paper or oatmeal paper make wonderful backgrounds.
* When attaching projects to the bulletin board, use pins or staples to attach the paper instead of tacks. The appearance is much neater.
* Use paper to cover and label storage boxes in the classroom.
* Use mural paper cut in large pieces to do individual, large-scale work.
* Household papers, such as waxed paper and freezing paper, are always good to have available in a classroom.

C. SUGGESTIONS FOR DISPLAY

For a long time, good teachers have been using displays or exhibits to point up good ideas, and to give meaning beyond vocal communication. Many people are able to grasp ideas more readily if confronted by visual aids in the form of pictures, graphs or diagrams; so there is a definite need for the display.

The display aids considerably in teaching because it motivates and inspires the child with varied ideas and materials, known and unknown. They encourage creativity, and give an opportunity to exhibit individual and group work. An exhibit also adds attractiveness to areas that might otherwise be considered "eyesores."

However, in order to be purposeful, the completed display, whether it be for social studies, science or arithmetic, must be thought out and planned so that the end result is a work of art.

One need not be an artist to obtain this end. It is hoped that the following suggestions will aid in the organization, function and general design of the exhibit.

1. Good Places to Exhibit

* Permanent Bulletin Boards
* Unused Wall Areas
* Unused Corners
* Folding Screens
* Tables
* Window Ledges
* Showcases
* Doors
* Boxes
* From the Ceiling

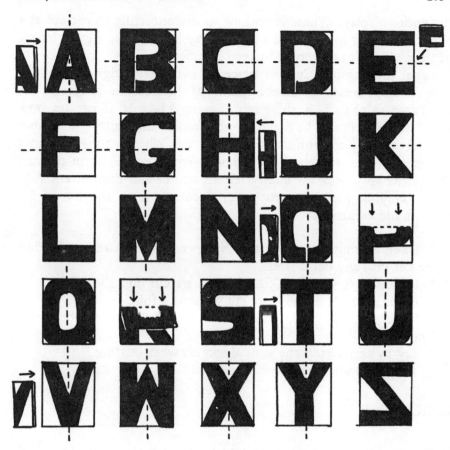

Figure 11-1

If lighting is poor, take advantage of artificial lighting for effectiveness or attempt to find an area that has good lighting. Choose a desirable location for the exhibit: one that is accessible to the greatest number of people.

The best way to attract attention to the exhibit is to establish a focal point. Plan the design with regard to line, area, shape and balance. Whenever possible, enhance the display through a variety of textures (paper, burlap, cork, screen, rope, string) and lights and darks. A mat behind or under objects is always in good taste. Gray or black should preferably be used for mats.

Pictures should fit their spaces. Do not attempt to put a huge picture in a small area. Also, tack materials so they become part of the entire display. (There is nothing so disconcerting to the eye as a picture flapping in the wind.) If a display has been up a great length of time, check it at intervals to keep it intact.

Label the exhibit. Cut-out letters or manuscript signs, no matter how simply done, become a point of interest in a display. A Cut-Paper Alphabet is shown in Figure 11-1. It illustrates how impressive letters can be made by just folding and cutting the paper in a certain way to form the required letters. When cutting out paper letters has been mastered, experiment with paper cut in unusual shapes. Make short and squatty letters, or tall and thin letters. Add paint, crayon, pastels or cut-paper decorations to the letters for interest and emphasis.

* When cutting letters, start with paper squares or rectangles that are cut into any equal sizes.
* Letters B, C, D, E, F, G, K, P and R are cut on a short fold.
* Letters J, L, N, S and Z are cut without a fold.
* Letters A, H, M, O, Q, T, I, U, V, W, X and Y are cut on a long fold.
* Try to keep letters the same thickness when cutting.
* THINK the letter while it is being cut.

D. RECIPES

The reader has probably realized by now that I have eliminated any suggestions for the use of ceramics in this book. This was done intentionally. Clay work will always be an important part of the art program and, as such, it is assumed that when the opportunity arises, the inclusion of clay work will add greatly to the quality of the curriculum.

However, this book has been geared to ordinary classroom teaching and, in most cases, the cost of the kiln for firing the clay would be prohibitive, even though the actual cost of the clay is minimal. Therefore, this chapter will deal specifically with easy, class-made products that can be prepared from materials that are easy to come by, can be purchased at a nominal fee or can be donated by parents. These products can be modeled or sculpted, and they will self dry; thus, a kiln is not needed.

Although a substitute process can never really equal the merits of clay, the children will at least be able to benefit from the procedure of handling and working in a pliable, three-dimensional medium.

Hopefully, you will be able to try all or some of these recipes in your classroom.

1. Winter Recipes

White Christmas Spray

1/2 cup white kitchen cleanser
1 cup water

In a jar, mix white cleanser and water. Shake well and place in spray gun for use.

Snow

1/3 package of soap flakes

Add enough water to make a thick paste. Beat with egg beater. Use at once.

2. Finger-Painting Recipes

Finger Paint

1/4 cup laundry starch
cold water
3 cups boiling water
1/2 cup soap flakes
1 tsp. glycerine or alum

Mix starch and water into a smooth paste. Add boiling water and cook 1/2 minute. Stir in soap and beat until creamy. Last, add the color and alum or glycerine.

Finger Paint

1 cup liquid starch
1 tsp. powdered paint

Place both ingredients in a jar and shake mixture thoroughly.

3. Recipes for Modeling

Salt Sculpture

4 cups flour
1 cup salt
1 1/2 cups water

Mix above materials. Sculpt shape. Allow several days to dry, then paint and shellac.

Sawdust Clay for Covering Objects

4 cups sawdust
1 1/2 cups wallpaper paste

1/4 cup plaster of Paris

Add enough water to dry ingredients to make a stiff mixture. This is excellent for covering an area or making a relief map.

Salt Sculpture

2 cups salt
2/3 cups water
1 cup starch
1/2 cup cold water

Heat salt and water for about 4 minutes. Add starch and then water. Stir. Remove from heat, cool, and sculpt. Allow several days to dry, then paint and shellac.

Wallpaper Paste — Sawdust — Plaster of Paris Clay

1 part wallpaper paste
4 parts sawdust
2 parts plaster of Paris

Mix above ingredients. Add enough water to model. Leave in natural state, or paint and decorate.

Simple Clay

19 parts clay flour
1 part (yellow) dextrin

Mix together and use as regular clay. It does not need firing, so when the product made is thoroughly dry, it can be painted with tempera and then shellacked.

Crepe-Paper Clay

1 fold crepe paper
1 cup flour
1 tblsp. salt

Cut the crepe paper into small pieces. Place in a large container and add enough water to cover. Let the paper soak for about an hour in the water until most of it is absorbed into the water. Then pour off the excess water

and start to add small quantities of the flour and salt until the mixture is the consistency of clay and the color of the paper has been blended with the flour, and not streaked. Shape forms and let them dry. The pieces are already colored, but can be preserved by shellacking them.

Salt and Flour Dough

2 pints flour
1 pint salt
water — food coloring (if desired)

Mix the flour and salt together. Add enough water to the dry mixture to make into modeling material. Dry and paint with tempera if not already colored.

Sawdust Sculpture

Mix 1 part each of sawdust, flour and water until the mixture forms a dough.
Place mixture on cardboard or aluminum foil and mold into the desired shape.
Allow 2 or 3 days for drying. Sand the completed object with sandpaper to smooth. Stain or shellac to finish.

Asbestos-Powder Modeling Material

6 pints asbestos (purchase from lumber yard)

1 pint wallpaper paste

Mix asbestos and wallpaper paste together. Add water to moisten. Model the material by pulling from the middle area instead of adding pieces. Allow several days for drying, then paint and shellac.

Easy Modeling Material

2 cups soap flakes
Equal amounts of Kleenex tissues or paper napkins

Mix the soap flakes and the torn paper. Add enough water to make into suitable modeling material. Allow to dry thoroughly, then paint and shellac.

Sawdust and Glue Clay

Dampen a quantity of sawdust with water. Then add white glue until it is stiff enough to model. Wet fingers frequently while working with the sawdust clay. When modeling is complete, let dry for several days, then paint and shellac or spray with clear shellac.

Salt and Cornstarch Beads

Brown in pan 2 tablespoons of salt until it cracks. Add 1 tablespoon of cornstarch and a little water. Boil 2 minutes — stirring constantly. Add food coloring.

When cool, roll the mixture into balls and stick a long pin or wire through the balls. Allow to dry at least overnight, then decorate.

Clay Dough

1 cup flour
1/2 cup salt
1/2 cup water

Mix ingredients. Then shape into forms. Place forms in 225° oven, and bake several hours to harden. Paint and decorate when cool.

Bread Dough

3 slices white bread
3 tblsp. white glue
And . . .
1 tsp. glycerine
                or
1 tblsp. white shoe polish
                or
3 drops lemon juice

Remove crusts from the bread. Tear bread into little pieces. Add glue plus 1 of the 3 items mentioned above. Now put a small quantity of lotion on the fingers and mix the materials together, then sculpt a shape. To prevent shrinkage, coat the completed object with a mixture of white glue and water. Place in 350° oven 3-5 minutes. Remove from oven, cool and paint with oils or acrylics. Dough keeps many weeks if refrigerated.

Hints, Suggestions and Recipes

Baking Soda and Cornstarch Dough

2 cups Baking Soda
1 cup cornstarch
1 1/4 cups cold water

Mix above ingredients until smooth. Heat and bring to a boil until the mixture resembles mashed potatoes. Transfer to foil and cover. Knead when cool. Let the shape dry several days, then paint and decorate.

Make Believe Cookies

4 cups flour
1 cup salt

Mix the flour and salt. Add water to moisten the dough. Roll the dough into flat pieces, cut into shapes. Make designs with sharp-pointed tools. Put a hole in the shape for hanging. Place aside to dry, then decorate and shellac.

4. Recipes for Sculpting

Plaster of Paris — Sand — Zonolite

1 part sand
2 parts plaster of Paris
3 parts Zonolite (from lumber supply co.)

Mix dry ingredients together. Add water to moisten. Pour into empty milk carton. Place aside to dry several days. Then remove carton. Carve and paint.

Cement and Sand

1 part cement   (first 3 items
1 part sand   from lumber
3 parts Zonolite   supply co.)
water

Mix dry ingredients together. Add water to make pliable. Pour mixture into empty milk cartons and allow to dry several days. When dry, carve and decorate.

Clay Powder and Plaster of Paris

4 parts clay powder
2 parts plaster of Paris
water

Mix dry ingredients, then add water to make thick consistency. Pour into empty milk carton and allow to dry several days. When dry, carve with old knives, chisels, nail files.

Glossary of Terms

Abstract	A work of art using lines, shapes and colors, without reference to colors.
Acrylics	Water-thinned, plastic-based paints that are extremely brilliant in color and most durable.
Antiquing	Giving a quality of being ancient, or of great age.
Applique	Cutting figures out of one material and applying them upon another.
Base relief	Sculpture in low relief in which the figures project only slightly from the background.
Batik	A method of printing cloth using a wax deposit in the desired pattern of the fabric.
Bleeding	To run or flow, one color into another.
Blending	To have no perceptible separation, e.g., when sea and sky seem to blend.
Brayer	A small roller for inking plates manually.
Brush	An instrument consisting of bristles, hair or the like, set in or attached to a handle and used for painting, cleaning, polishing, rubbing, etc.
Casein	An adhesive and binding material made from the curd of soured skim milk.
Collage	An abstract composition employing a variety of materials such as newspapers, string and stones, with lines and colors supplied by the artist.
Composition	Organization or grouping of the different parts of a work of art so as to achieve a unified whole.
Construction	The arrangement of two or more parts to form a unit.

Contrast	Opposition or juxtaposition of different forms, lines or colors in a work of art to intensify each other's properties and produce a more dynamic expression.
Crayon etching	A process of making designs or pictures in a crayon drawing by scraping or scratching away the crayon wax.
Crayon glazing	Covering a surface with a thin layer of almost transparent crayon color, which gives a smooth, lustrous coating.
Diluted paint	Paint thinned by the addition of water.
Dry brush	A brush almost entirely void of paint.
Encaustic	Painted with wax colors that have been fixed with heat.
Etching	To cut, bite or corrode a design in furrows with an acid or the like. When this is charged with ink it will give a printed impression on paper.
Finger paint	A thickened type of paint, which is applied to a surface with hands, fingers and elbows.
Fixative	A gummy liquid sprayed on drawing or pastel to prevent blurring.
Frame	An enclosing border or case for a picture.
Gesso	Gypsum or plaster of Paris, prepared with glue for use on a surface for painting.
Graphic	Drawing, engraving, etching, painting and other arts involving the use of lines and strokes to express or convey ideas in terms of forms.
India ink	A liquid ink made of lampblack mixed with a binding material.
Laminate	To construct by placing layer upon layer.
Loom	An apparatus for weaving yarn or thread into a woven fabric.
Macrame	Ornamental work made by knotting thread or cord into patterns.

Manila paper	Strong, light-brown paper derived originally from Manila hemp, but now also from wood-pulp substitute not of equal strength.
Marbleized	A marbled appearance or pattern.
Masking	A covering that conceals or protects a material while another material is applied over it.
Mobile	A hanging construction or sculpture of delicately balanced movable parts, which describes rhythmic patterns through the motion of its parts.
Monoprint	A single print taken from a simple painted plate.
Mosaic	A picture or decoration made of small pieces of stone, glass or clay tile of different colors, inlaid to form a design.
Muted	Not pronounced.
Neutralized	Without hue.
Newsprint	Paper used for or made to print newspaper.
Oaktag	A stiff, sturdy paper.
Oil paint	Paint with an oil base.
Opaque	Impenetrable to light; not able to transmit light.
Overlap	To extend over or cover a part of something.
Palette	A thin board or tablet on which painters mix their colors.
Papier mache	A substance made of pulped paper or paper pulp mixed with paste and other materials; or layers of paper pasted and pressed together, which becomes hard and strong when dry.
Pastels	A kind of dried paste used like crayons, made of pigments ground with chalk and compounded with gum water.
Plasticene	A clay blended with oil to remain in a plastic, pliable state.
Plate	A sheet of some type of material used to print from and yielding a printed impression.

Pointillism	A method of painting; an offshoot of French Impressionism in which luminosity is produced by laying on the colors in points or small dots of unmixed color, which are blended by the eye.
Polymer medium	Fine particles of acrylic plastic resin suspended in water. Evaporation of the water creates a clear, strong, flexible binder that is highly adhesive and immediately becomes waterproof.
Poster paint	A water-based paint which is opaque, flat and smooth when dry.
Print	A design or picture printed from an engraved or otherwise prepared block or plate.
Realistic painting	A painting executed to represent things as they really are.
Repeat	A duplicate or reproduction of something.
Resist	To withstand the action or effect of a substance.
Rice paper	An oriental paper consisting of the pith of certain plants, cut and pressed into thin paper sheets.
Rubbing	A reproduction of an incised or sculptured surface made by laying paper or the like upon it and rubbing with some marking substance.
Sand casting	To produce a shape by casting plaster of Paris in a sand mold.
Scoring	A cut or scratch into the surface of a material, which can be curved or straight. Folding the scored piece allows it to take lights and cast shadows that create relief pieces. A fold can be made on a curve.
Scratchboard	A drawing board coated with a smooth, chalky surface; when coated with ink the artist can scratch the surface with a sharp tool and produce a wood engraving effect.
Sculpting	The fine art of forming figures or designs in relief, in intaglio, or in the round by cutting marble, wood, etc.
Sealer	Anything which effectively closes or locks in a material.

Sgraffito	Decoration produced on pottery or ceramic by scratching through a surface or plaster or glazing to reveal a different color beneath.
Shading	Degrees of darkness and lightness in a picture.
Silk screen	A stencil process using fine cloths that have been painted with an impermeable coating except in areas where color is to be forced through onto paper, etc.
Sketch	A simple or hastily executed drawing or painting which gives essential features of a picture without the details.
Spatter	To scatter or dash in small particles or drops.
Squeegee	An implement edged with rubber or the like, for removing paint from a silk screen frame.
Stabile	A constructed piece in fixed position but usually with some moving parts.
Stencil	A thin sheet of cardboard or other material cut through in such a way as to reproduce a design when color is rubbed through it.
Stitchery	A particular mode of sewing with ornamental stitches.
Stipple	To paint or draw by means of dots or small touches.
Styrofoam	A trademark for a light resilient polystyrene plastic.
Symmetrical design	Correspondence in size, form and arrangement of parts on opposite sides of a plane, line or point.
Tempera	Painting with water-based paint called tempera paint.
Tesserae	Small bits of tile, stone, glass or any other miscellaneous materials used in doing mosaic work.
Textile	Any material that is woven.
Texture	The structure of the surface of any work of art or the simulation of the surface structure of the skin, garment, etc.
Transparent	A picture or design on glass or some translucent substance, made visible by light shining through from behind.
Unify	To make into one.

Velour paper	Paper with the texture of velvet.
Veneer	To give a superficially fair appearance by adding materials to the outside surface of something.
Warp	Yarn placed lengthwise in a loom, across the weft or woof, and interlaced.
Wash	A liquid with which something is washed, wetted, colored, overspread, etc.
Woof	Yarn that travels from selvage to selvage in a loom, interlacing with the warp.

Index